# A BEAUTIFUL MIND

## THE LANGUAGE MISSING FROM YOUR HEALING JOURNEY

Olivier Christian

**A Beautiful Mind**
**The language missing from your healing journey**
**Olivier Christian**

First published in Australia by Olivier Christian 2022

A catalogue record for this book is available from the National Library of Australia

ISBN: 978-0-6484230-9-6 (pbk)
ISBN: 978-0-6456271-0-7 (ebk)

Typesetting and design by Publicious Book Publishing
www.publicious.com.au



**Disclaimer:** in the unlikely event that it comes to light that another's rights have been unconsciously breached in this publication, changes will be made in later editions.

# ABOUT ME

My name is Olivier Christian. I grew up in Sydney, Australia. In 2020 I went through many traumatic experiences with both my physical and mental health. I have since decided to dedicate my life to helping those who suffer in the way that I did. I spend my days running my mental health business, A Beautiful Mind & Co.

If you would like to order any of our Mental Health Packages or other products, such as our Inner Child Healing Cards and Daily Mental Health Checker Notepads, please visit www.abeautifulmindandco.com.au or visit our Instagram page, @abeautifulmindandco

I am also a trained performer and very passionate about the benefits music has on our mental and emotional health. I teach singing and acting. Whilst highlighting how trauma sits in the voice, I navigate my students toward unlocking their full resonance, which is often detained by their conditioning. If you would like to enquire about lessons, please visit: olivierssingingstudio.com.au or visit us on Instagram @oliviers_singing_studio.

Helping and coaching others is why I am here.

# WHY I WROTE THIS BOOK

Hello. Hi. Yes, I'm here. I'm breathing. I showed up. I am not on time but I am alive. I followed through. Potentially for the first time. It was always something I struggled with, so this is big for me.

Prior to this year, I was blinded by the fog of my trauma but now that I have broken free and knowingly stepped away from much of it, I want to help you do the same. We all deserve to fully show up for ourselves.

I wrote this book while fighting off physical illness. I'd been bedridden for six months and sick for over two years. No doctor could tell me what was wrong. I was constantly misdiagnosed and poked at. My body had betrayed me and my mind followed shortly after.

While physically ill, I managed to get into an abusive relationship. It was the biggest, sweetest cherry on top of a whole fuck-load of shit-filled cake. I know. I should make a movie. It will come. So juicy.

Although that particular chapter is not really of much relevance to my story, throughout my two-year-long nervous breakdown, I did notice I had gotten out of a very abusive 'relationship' with somebody else. And later, as I discovered, with myself.

I had awoken.

This shit-filled cake had great purpose. It wasn't just a 'light bulb moment', it was like seven million light bulbs in the shape of an arrow. All were done with being dimmed. All were pointing right toward my biggest fears and saying, "This is the answer you are looking for."

It was this or death by heartbreak. Those were my two options. Forced clarity through an outpouring of self-neglect.

My Jenga home. All. Came. Tumbling. Down.

Blind spots in regard to self-love were no longer hidden in the dark. My worth was no longer crammed into spaces it didn't quite fit.

With this light, everything became clear and hopeful. Its enchanting familiarity was encouraging me to rebuild but, this time, not without proper thought or caution.

All I had to do was understand each piece of trauma that was disguising itself as a self-protection mechanism. I had to dispose of the jagged and limiting self-beliefs I'd been taught during my time here on Planet Trauma. And, I had to place new, self-made and helpful beliefs in their God-allocated position.

How easy.

How chill.

With this new-found awareness of the neglected grief and trauma sitting within me, I was eager to do the very triggering and painstaking work to acknowledge and heal all of it. Inevitably, it became clear to me that, prior my crash, I did not know myself or love myself. Nor was I taught how to escape the self moulded by expectations and society. I was stuck living someone else's life; one created by their misplaced sense of fear.

My. Self.

We are born ourselves. So, in order to know myself and be myself, I needed to rediscover the self who was not yet exposed to trauma – the untouched version of myself. I needed to find my way back to the 'me' who had never been bullied, shamed, rejected or had love withheld. I had been unknowingly beaten and distorted by societal norms, the self-hating, the fear-ridden and those who thought changing me was safer than acknowledging me. I wasn't going to allow them all to discourage me from finding the little boy whose unpronounced vocabulary knew of nothing beyond love. I decided to fight like hell for the inner environment in which I was born to thrive.

Sometimes, wisdom just hits us differently. We have to hear it at specific moments in our journey to get its full effect. This is usually when we need those words for our survival. Often, wisdom is white noise. I recall not truly hearing much at all. Even the things I might hear now and find groundbreakingly profound and brilliantly liberating would have had zero impact on me.

A few years ago, this book would have translated into something more along the lines of 'Stuff the patriarchy blah. Stuff society blah blah. Love your blah self. Be woke. Love is the answer. Blah blah blah.' But now, this is the lame language that saves me day after day. Its truth counteracts with my unhelpful internal monologue and overrides my demons.

The thing is you can't force words into somebody's subconscious. You have either finished faking it or you are yet to be open to the suffering that comes when we acknowledge our past wounds. This acknowledgment summons us to our humanity.

In truth, you have to choose to run into a burning building. Then, whether your healing comes from awareness, defeat, overflow, a breakdown or intrigue, you're facing scarcity. Therefore, you are open for it to find its way to you. Let me be very clear about one thing – your reset always belonged to you. I promise there is grace in the struggle.

This book is my love letter to you.

I aspire for my writing to be an invitation to your own healing. However, it is up to the individual if they choose to RSVP.

Together. we can analyse and soften harsh beliefs. We can then create new beliefs; those in which I am convinced humanity will benefit from carrying. My goal is to influence a mindset of compassion; one we can all soak and heal in.

I became tired of sadness and sickness. I had no interest in staying in the space of disbelief that this could happen to me. Now, all I feel is a strong need to make it all mean something. This book is that something.

I did something.

I showed up.

And, in the process, created a beautiful mind.

# INTRODUCTION

Repairing yourself is always going to be an option.

Healing is a fulltime job. It is also the most challenging, yet rewarding job. Life can truly begin once we decide to love ourselves without condition. No more numbing. The only time we run is if it is toward our pain.

A lack of awareness for our wounds is the destructive force in modern society. Let us question everything we thought we knew and remember to always stay curious.

If you are reading this book, you're now doing the healing work. Congratulations! What a beautiful place for you to be; the stage prior to internal tranquillity.

# HOW TO USE THIS BOOK

When I wrote A Beautiful Mind, I did so as the moment took me. Each page features my thoughts or feelings on any particular day throughout my healing journey.

There is no manufactured order. I was very deliberate, as I was editing the book, to maintain a more organic 'flow'. Our healing is not linear. It is not structured. It is strange and, more often than not, makes no sense. To the outsider, it may seem fragmented or disjointed. To the broken, I aspire it to be relatable and truthful.

A Beautiful Mind details the path I took in my healing. Some pages may resonate with you. Others may not. That is okay.

Each page contains the following:

1. A general statement to encourage further thought.
2. An anecdote or reflection from my lived experience.
3. An affirmation linking back to the statement and summing up the overall message.

You may choose to read this book from beginning to end. You may bookmark and return to those pages that resonated with you. Or you may decide to open the book at random when your head hurts.

However you choose to read about my journey, my hope is that it brings you peace, comfort and health.

Be sure to share your favourite quotes and tag @ abeautifulmindandco so we can share them on our social media.

THE BEST WAY TO TRULY LOVE SOMEBODY IS TO UNDERSTAND THEIR TRAUMA.

---

THAT GOES FOR YOURSELF, TOO. ONCE YOU UNDERSTAND YOUR TRAUMA AND KNOW WHAT IS HAPPENING INSIDE, YOU CAN DEVELOP THE SELF-SOOTHING LANGUAGE YOUR NERVOUS SYSTEM REQUIRES. HEALING BEGINS WHEN WE FIND THE WORDS MISSING INSIDE OF US.

---

Affirmation: I choose deep awareness of my trauma in order to seek out the magical words it requires to rest.

LET'S FOCUS ON THE BEAUTY
THAT INHERITS THIS EARTH.

---

I CAN CHOOSE WHAT TO LOOK AT,
JUST LIKE I CAN CHOOSE TO SHUT
MY EYES TO LIFE'S BLESSINGS.

---

Affirmation: I choose to seek
all the beauty on earth.

WE SUFFER SO MUCH IN IMAGINATION, NOT A WHOLE LOT IN REALITY.

---

HOW FUNNY. AFTER ALL THAT CARNAGE, THEY REALLY WERE JUST WORDS GOING THROUGH MY HEAD.

---

Affirmation: I choose to differentiate between my thoughts and reality.

PAINFUL EVENTS ARE FIVE PER CENT EVENT AND NINETY-FIVE PER CENT REACTION.

---

MANY OF US HAVE BEEN CONDITIONED TO REACT WILDLY. TRY VIEWING EVERYTHING AS A HASSLE AND REJECT A DISASTROUS OUTLOOK ON LIFE'S INCONVENIENCES. LET'S CHOOSE A LITTLE DIFFERENTLY TODAY.

---

Affirmation: I choose to tame my reactions.

MY LOVE LANGUAGE IS
LISTENING TO MY GUT.

---

ALL OTHER NOISE EITHER
DOESN'T MAKE SENSE OR
HURTS MY HEART A LITTLE.

---

Affirmation: I choose to cancel
the noise and follow my gut.

LET US NEVER AGAIN VIEW SOMEONE ELSE'S LACK OF INVESTMENT AS AN OPPORTUNITY TO PROVE WE ARE ENOUGH.

---

BECAUSE I AM DIVINE, I DO NOT NEED TO PROVE THAT.

---

Affirmation: I choose to love me like nobody else's business.

DON'T WARRANT UNWORTHY PEOPLE SUCH A PRESTIGE POSITION IN YOUR HEART AND MIND.

---

SOMETIMES LOVING OTHERS AT ARM'S LENGTH IS WHAT IS REQUIRED FOR A HEALTHY RELATIONSHIP WITH YOURSELF.

---

Affirmation: I choose to be thoughtful with where I place my love.

WE WILL STEP INTO OUR POWER AND ADMIRE THOSE WHO ARE INSPIRED TO FOLLOW.

---

DO NOT FEAR LEAVING ANYONE BEHIND WHEN STEPPING OUT OF YOUR TRAUMA AND INTO YOUR HIGHER SELF. WHOEVER IS READY TO FOLLOW, WILL. IT WAS NEVER UP TO YOU.

---

Affirmation: I choose to actively strip myself of fear.

WE CAN NO LONGER CONTOUR OURSELVES TO BE WHAT OTHERS CRAVE. DESIRE FOR SELF AND FOR AUTHENTICITY INVOLVES FAR TOO MUCH LONGING.

---

YOUR CONDITIONING OF ME DOESN'T INTEREST ME. I AM TOO UNIQUE FOR SUPPRESSION.

---

Affirmation: I choose to set my authentic self free.

## REJECTION IS A TRANSFORMATIVE AND UNIVERSAL EXPERIENCE.

---

MY HEART HURTS A LITTLE LESS
EACH TIME I WELCOME MY FEAR
OF REJECTION WITH OPEN ARMS.
NOW I KNOW; IF THE PAIN PERSISTS,
THE CHILD WITHIN ME IS ASKING
FOR A REMINDER THAT THEY ARE
ENOUGH. THEY ARE TELLING ME
THAT A BELIEF I HOLD ABOUT MYSELF
STILL NEEDS TO BE UNLEARNED.

---

Affirmation: I choose to believe I am enough.

LET US MAKE THE EFFORT TO APOLOGISE EVERY DAY FOR THE SELF-VIOLENCE WE TURN A BLIND EYE TO.

---

HEY! IT'S ME. YOUR INNER CHILD. STOP ABANDONING ME. I AM TRUTHFUL. I AM HONEST. I AM HURTING. I MATTER. PLEASE LISTEN TO ME.

---

Affirmation: I choose to stop people-pleasing and listen instead to myself.

IGNITE YOUR JOY BY LIFTING A MAGNIFYING GLASS TO WHAT THE REST OF THE WORLD TAKES FOR GRANTED.

---

TREES, BLUE SKY, SUN ON MY SKIN AND A SMILE FROM A STRANGER ARE ALL I NEED TO SURVIVE IN THIS LIFETIME.

---

Affirmation: I choose not to over-complicate my life.

## SOCIETY IS A WATCHDOG THAT WILL SNIFF OUT EVEN A GLIMPSE OF INAUTHENTICITY.

---

INAUTHENTICITY IS REPELLENT TO OUR SOCIETY AND THE OPPOSITE OF ATTRACTION. CATCH YOURSELF OUT EACH TIME YOU SELF-ABANDON. YOU'LL ALWAYS STRUGGLE TO BE LIKE THEM BUT, WHEN YOU 'DO YOU', YOU ARE THE SUPREME.

---

Affirmation: I choose to be fully myself.

I WANT YOU TO FEED
THE GOOD FOR THE REST
OF YOUR TIME HERE.

---

YOUR ANGELS ARE MALNOURISHED. GRATITUDE WILL KEEP THEM ALIVE. THAT HEALTHY MINDSET IS RIGHT THERE IN FRONT OF YOU, WAITING TO BE TAKEN.

---

Affirmation: I choose to feed my angels, not my demons.

WHATEVER YOU CHOOSE
TO WATER WILL GROW.

---

LESS THIRST-TRAPS, MORE QUENCHING
OF YOUR DEHYDRATED SENSE OF SELF.

---

Affirmation: I choose to water that
which deserves not to starve.

IT'S TIME TO INTERROGATE OUR NERVOUS SYSTEM RESPONSES. THEY ARE AN INVITATION TO A DEEPER WOUND.

---

YOUR REACTION COULD DO WITH SOME TAMING. IDENTIFY AND DECONSTRUCT THE WOUND BEHIND THIS PAIN-DRIVEN RESPONSE. SOMETHING IS BEING TRIGGERED HERE. SEEK THE TRUTH.

---

Affirmation: I choose to get curious about my reactivity.

ZERO SUM THINKING
IS OUR DOWNFALL.

---

YOU MEAN TO TELL ME THAT IF YOU WIN THE LOTTO, MY LIFE DOESN'T CHANGE AT ALL? HOW DARE YOU.

---

Affirmation: I choose not to see others advancing as a personal loss.

I RAN HEADFIRST INTO THE PAIN BECAUSE IT WAS THE ONLY WAY I COULD GO TO ITS DEPTHS AND NAVIGATE IT TO THE LIGHT.

---

IT WAS LIKE RUNNING INTO MY COLLAPSING HOME TO SAVE MY CHILD. IT WAS TERRIFYING. IT WAS ALSO LIFESAVING, HEROIC AND CONCLUSIVE. A NEW CHAPTER CAN BEGIN. NOW THAT I HAVE A DEEPER UNDERSTANDING OF MY PAIN, I CAN CHOOSE DIFFERENTLY.

---

Affirmation: I choose not to run from my wounds.

## PRACTICE BEING YOURSELF EVERY DAY.

---

IT IS SO EASY TO FALL BACK INTO THE HABITS OF YOUR CONDITIONING. EACH MORNING, BE CONSCIOUS OF WHO YOU DECIDE TO BE AS YOU ENTER THE WORLD. I ALWAYS RECOMMEND YOU CHOOSE YOU.

---

Affirmation: I choose to be my light, kind self.

HERE I AM. BREATHING THROUGH THE PAIN, SITTING IN THE DISCOMFORT, HOPING IT WON'T BE THIS BAD NEXT TIME.

---

KEEP SITTING. KEEP BREATHING. GET COMFORTABLE IN YOUR DISCOMFORT FOR THIS IS WHERE THE MAGIC HAPPENS.

---

Affirmation: I choose to outgrow my pain.

REGARDLESS OF THE ISSUE, I CANNOT ARTICULATE ABOUT ANYTHING BRAVER THAN SOMEONE WHO IS WILLING TO STARE THEIR SHAME IN THE FACE AND ACTIVELY SEEK HELP.

---

WITHOUT THERAPY, I WOULD BE STUCK, LIKE MANY, IN A YOUNG-MINDED STATE OF TRAUMA. NOT MOVING. NOT EVOLVING. NOT PUBLISHING BOOKS. YOU DESERVE TO DROP THE EGO. YOU DESERVE TO BELIEVE YOU ARE WORTHY OF RECEIVING HELP. YOUR BODY IS QUITE LITERALLY BEGGING YOU FOR IT.

---

Affirmation: I choose to be brave and ask for help when needed.

THERE IS SO MUCH
BEAUTY IN BEING GIVEN
THE OPPORTUNITY
TO START OVER.

---

I WOULDN'T TAKE BACK THE PAIN. SURE,
I AM EXHAUSTED BUT I AM FINALLY FREE.

---

Affirmation: I choose to let
my pain transform me.

DRAG ME THROUGH THE FIRE AND I'LL CALL MYSELF THE CHOSEN ONE.

---

A REMINDER TO SHIFT YOUR PERSPECTIVE.

---

Affirmation: I choose to find my blessings in negative situations.

YOUR ANXIETY IS JUST A FALSE ALARM THAT TAKES TIME TO DISARM. YOU'RE DOING REALLY WELL.

---

I UNDERSTAND YOUR DESIRE TO JUST PULL THE PLUG. IT WILL GET BETTER. IT ALREADY HAS.

---

Affirmation: I choose to keep going.

RADICAL ACCEPTANCE
IS FUCKING SEXY.

---

TO MAKE SOMEONE FEEL SAFE IS THE GREATEST GIFT YOU CAN GIVE. GIVE THAT SHIT TO EVERYONE.

---

Affirmation: I choose to make all around me feel safe and secure.

PLOT TWIST: I LOVE ME.

---

NO COMMENT. EXCEPT A COMMENT:
TREAT YOURSELF, LOVE YOURSELF, FEEL
YOURSELF AND BE PROUD OF YOURSELF.

---

Affirmation: Today, I choose to love
my ugly even more than my pretty.

## LOVE WHOLE-HEARTEDLY AND HAVE NO EXPECTATION OF PERFECTION.

---

I DON'T WANT YOU TO BE PERFECT. I WANT YOU TO BE TRUTHFUL. SHOW ME YOUR IMPERFECTIONS AND LET ME ADORE EVERY PART OF THEM.

---

Affirmation: I choose understanding over judgement.

YOUR INNER CHILD IS THE DEEPEST PART OF YOUR WOUND. HEAL THEM AND YOU'LL HEAL YOUR WHOLE SELF. HEAL YOUR WHOLE SELF AND YOU'LL HEAL OTHERS.

---

A LOT OF US SUBCONSCIOUSLY HOLD ON TO OLD PAIN. THAT IS THE CHILD WITHIN YOU STATING ITS FUNDAMENTAL NEED FOR RECONNECTION THROUGH COMPASSION. FEED YOUR INNER CHILD BY UNPACKING PAST TRAUMA AND TELLING THEM THEY ARE NOW SAFE.

---

Affirmation: I choose reconnection to my inner child.

THINGS YOUR INNER CHILD
MAY NEED TO HEAR:
I AM LISTENING TO YOU.
I'M REALLY SORRY FOR WHAT
HAPPENED TO YOU.
YOU DIDN'T DESERVE THE PAIN.
YOU ARE SAFE NOW.
THE ADULT HAS ARRIVED;
THE CHILD CAN NOW REST.
I ACCEPT YOU AND LOVE YOU
UNCONDITIONALLY.
I'LL NEVER LEAVE YOU.
IT WASN'T YOUR FAULT.

---

Tip: Look at a photo of your younger self while making the statements above, or better yet, go to www.abeautifulmindandco.com.au and get your own pack of Inner Child Healing Cards.

---

Affirmation: I choose to love and nourish my inner child.

IT IS EMOTIONALLY IMPOSSIBLE TO FEAR THE PAST. MAYBE IT IS TIME WE TOYED WITH THE IDEA THAT THE SAME GOES FOR OUR FUTURE.

---

FEARING YOUR SHADOW IS OVERRATED. LET'S TRY SOMETHING NEW TODAY.

---

Affirmation: I choose release.

IF YOU'VE PERMITTED SOMEONE TO BE YOUR EMOTIONAL CENTRE OF GRAVITY, YOU'VE SELF-ABANDONED.

---

MANY OF US HAVE AN UNDERLYING BELIEF THAT WE ARE UNLOVABLE. THIS MAKES US ACT OUT. PLEASE REMIND YOURSELF DAILY THAT YOU WERE BORN ENOUGH AND ARE WORTHY, SIMPLY BY BEING.

---

Affirmation: I choose to listen to the most important voice – my own.

WE HATE REJECTION BUT LOVE TO REJECT OURSELVES.

---

INSTEAD OF ELIMINATING, TRY LISTENING TO THAT VOICE THAT SAYS, "MAYBE I DESERVE MORE THAN THIS."

---

Affirmation: I choose to nourish my self-esteem by listening to myself.

I KNOW YOU'D RATHER LAUGH AT ME BUT I'LL LAUGH WITH YOU UNTIL YOU'RE READY TO TAKE THE NEXT STEP.

---

SIDE WITH UNDERSTANDING, EVEN WHEN SOMEBODY'S PAIN TRIES TO OFFEND YOU. YOU HAVE THE POTENTIAL TO BE SO KIND.

---

Affirmation: I choose kindness, always.

PEOPLE MAY VIEW YOUR SELF-LOVE AS A THREAT BECAUSE THEY KNOW THEY DON'T POSSESS SUCH BEAUTY.

---

KEEP SHINING ANYWAY. BRIGHTER AND BRIGHTER AND BRIGHTER. ONE DAY, THEY'LL TIRE OF GIVING THEMSELVES THAT LAST-PLACE RIBBON AND MAKE A CHANGE.

---

Affirmation: I choose to keep shining my bright, infectious light.

“WHY DID THIS HAPPEN TO ME?” IS FAR MORE WORK THAN “HOW DID THIS HAPPEN FOR ME?”

---

THERE IS GRACE IN EVERYTHING. I DECIDE TO VIEW CHAOS AS OPPORTUNITY.

---

Affirmation: I choose to move forward in life.

## THEIR WILD BELIEFS ARE SHAPED BY THEIR TRAUMA.

---

A NEGATIVE BELIEF FLOURISHES FROM THE SEEDS OF TRAUMA. IF THEY DO NOT UNDERSTAND THEIR TRAUMA, THEY MAY NOT HAVE THE CAPACITY TO UNDERSTAND WHY THEY HOLD SUCH LIMITING BELIEFS. AWARENESS IS POWER AND THE BEGINNING OF ALL POSITIVE CHANGE.

---

Affirmation: I choose to notice where my beliefs are resistant.

THE MOST DANGEROUS THING IN THE WORLD IS A PERSON WHO IS UNAWARE THEY ARE BLEEDING.

---

A LACK OF AWARENESS MEANS NO HEALING IS BEING DONE. NEGLECTED WOUNDS BLEED INTO THOSE YOU LOVE MOST AND WILL CONTINUE TO REOPEN IF YOU CHOOSE TO DO NOTHING. THIS IS THE SIGN YOU'VE BEEN LOOKING FOR; SPEAK TO SOMEONE.

---

Affirmation: I choose to be proactive with my healing, if not for me, for those I love most.

## I CHOOSE ME AND I WILL ALWAYS CHOOSE ME.

---

WHY WOULDN'T I? I AM DIVINE. I AM WORTH CHOOSING. I AM MY 'HAPPILY EVER AFTER'. LET US RID OURSELVES OF THE IDEA THAT WE MUST POUR FROM AN EMPTY CUP AND SUFFER IN ORDER TO BE WORTH ANYTHING. YOU ARE NO GOOD TO ANYONE IN A STATE OF SELF-LOATHING AND EXHAUSTION.

---

Affirmation: I choose me, myself and I.

YOU CAN WANT EVERYTHING IN THE WORLD BUT IF YOU DON'T FIND THE FIRE WITHIN TO FIGHT AND WORK, NOTHING WILL EVER EVENTUATE. TODAY'S THE DAY YOU CHASE YOUR DREAMS. THEY ARE RIGHT THERE IN FRONT OF YOU.

---

I GOT TIRED OF WISHING SO I STARTED DOING. NOW'S YOUR CHANCE. TAKE. ACTION.

---

Affirmation: I choose to work hard for the things I want.

YOUR LIGHT WILL ONLY IRRITATE THOSE WHO ARE UNHEALED.

---

BUY SOME GLASSES, BABY. I'M JUST GETTING STARTED.

---

Affirmation: I choose to exude my rays of happiness.

YOU'RE RICH AND BROKEN.
I'M SORRY YOU WERE TAUGHT
THAT THIS IS SUCCESS.

---

THOSE WHO DISREGARD THEIR HEALTH FOR THE DOLLAR ARE POORER THAN THEY'VE BEEN CONDITIONED TO BELIEVE. IF YOU DO NOT HAVE HEALTH, PEACE AND LOVE FOR SELF, YOU HAVE NOTHING. DO YOUR BEST TO ALIGN WHILE YOU'RE STILL HERE.

REALITY CHECK: YOU'RE TAKING NONE OF IT TO THE GRAVE.

TRUTH BOMB: THEY WILL REMEMBER YOUR SPIRIT, NOT THE CAR YOU DRIVE.

---

Affirmation: I choose to chase connection to self before tangible goods.

## ROCK BOTTOM IS OFTEN EXACTLY WHERE PEOPLE NEED TO BE.

---

I WILL NEVER AGAIN TRY TO SAVE ANYONE FROM ROCK BOTTOM. I UNDERSTAND ITS POWER AND PURPOSE. IT IS THE HARDEST THING PEOPLE WILL EVER GO THROUGH. IT IS THE MOST PAINFUL THING THEY WILL EVER EXPERIENCE. BUT IT IS THE BEST THING THAT CAN EVER HAPPEN TO THEM. AND IT IS THE ONLY WAY THEY CAN TRULY BE SET FREE AND EVOLVE. MARK MY WORDS: THE ONLY PERSON WHO CAN SAVE THEM, IS THEMSELVES.

---

Affirmation: I choose to let rock bottom happen to all those I love the most.

DO NOT ALLOW
THE DISCOMFORT OF PTSD
TO ALTER YOUR VIEW OF
LIFE. THOSE BEAUTIFUL
THINGS ARE NOT MEANT
TO BE SEEN IN GREY.

---

LOOK AROUND AT WHAT IS REAL.
DISCARD WHAT IS EITHER INTRUSIVE,
WRAPPED IN FEAR OR IN THE PAST.
THESE THINGS ARE EITHER LIES
OR NO LONGER YOUR TRUTH.

---

Affirmation: I choose to keep
rebuilding my mind.

SOCIETY TRAINS MEN TO FLATTEN THEIR FEMININITY.

---

SUPPRESSION IS NEVER HELPFUL. TRY EMBRACING WHAT YOU'VE BEEN TAUGHT IS 'FEMININE'. IT WILL USUALLY BE SOFT AND KIND, AND IT WILL GIFT YOU WITH THE EMOTIONAL CAPACITY YOU REQUIRE TO FEEL RELEASE.

---

Affirmation: I choose to be fully human by embracing both masculinity and femininity.

MY ABUSER WISHES THEY COULD REVEL IN THIS KIND OF SELF-LOVE.

---

WITHIN ME IS THE KIND OF EUPHORIA YOU'LL NEVER EXPERIENCE. I CHOSE ME WHEN YOU TOLD ME NO-ONE ELSE EVER WOULD. THAT IS SOMETHING YOU CAN NEVER TAKE AWAY.

---

Affirmation: I choose to continue giving myself the pep-talks I require.

## A TIP FOR TENSION HEADACHES:

---

STICK YOUR TONGUE OUT AS FAR AS YOU CAN FOR A RELEASE.

---

Affirmation: I choose to release.

YOU MAY BE OVER IT BUT IF YOUR THOUGHT PROCESS WAS AFFECTED, IT'S TIME TO WORK THROUGH IT.

---

I WANT EVERYONE TO KNOW THAT LIFE IS NOT FOR SUFFERING. LIFE IS FOR EXPLORING, UNDERSTANDING, LOVING, FORGIVING AND FREEING ONE'S SELF. TODAY IS THE DAY YOU WILL LOVE YOURSELF ENOUGH TO GET HELP. MAKE THAT CALL, BOOK IN THAT THERAPY SESSION, READ THE BOOKS AND DO THE WORK. RELEASE THE STIGMA AND SHAME. YOU'RE HUMAN. ALL HUMANS ARE DESERVING OF HELP AND HEALTH.

---

Affirmation: I choose high self-esteem.

EVEN WHEN SHIT HITS THE FAN, BE BRAVE ENOUGH TO KEEP SMILING.

---

I KNOW, IF THE WORST WERE EVER TO HAPPEN, YOU WOULD MAKE IT THROUGH. TOUGH TIMES ARE NEVER GOING TO BE PERMANENT. NEVER.

---

Affirmation: I choose peace in knowing nothing is permanent.

SOMETIMES, THE PEOPLE WHO ARE MEANT TO KEEP YOU SAFE DON'T KNOW HOW.

---

IT'S NOT THEIR FAULT THEY'VE BEEN CONDITIONED TO CHOOSE FEAR. IT IS A CONCRETE BELIEF SYSTEM THEY ARE TRAPPED IN. IT IS, HOWEVER, THEIR CHOICE TO REMAIN STUCK AND YOUR CHOICE TO DO THINGS DISSIMILARLY.

---

Affirmation: I choose to do whatever it takes to feel safe.

# A NOTE FOR THE DISSOCIATED

For the first twenty-six years of my life, I was stuck in a dissociative fantasy. This was the safe place I ran to when I felt so incredibly unsafe in real time. After many years of constant fantasising in my youth, it became clear to me – this place was *my* version of reality. My world. My fantasy. My truth. They were all one. The same. I'd always loved Disney so fantasy land was a fit for me. Right? But it was still real. I knew it was real. It had to be real. It was all I'd known.

Fantasy became my truth. I lost all control over what was real and what was in my head. This was how I survived but also how I lost myself. I was stuck here, unable to feel.

It was confronting when life threw its nastiness in my face. It was like a body-slam that woke me up for a second. I didn't know what was happening in those real moments. All I knew is that it was foreign and difficult. I know now I was being blessed with glimpses of feeling for the first time. I was being temporarily awoken. The words 'snap out of it' began to make sense. Thus, my intrigue for the outside world began, coupled as it was with the package deal of terror in facing my sobriety.

I was placed in the midst of absolute chaos. Traumatic events that damage our brains are the most difficult to overcome. However, if the fear wasn't so debilitating, it could never have demanded I face it.

The most difficult things often save us. Grace and divinity are the creators of pain. Pain was my saviour. I had been invited to escape my current life as a fully grown man who was stuck in a child-like state of trauma. I was saved from my fantasy. Saved from eternal emptiness and numbness. I would've never truly lived. I would've never known, nor seen, how my panting was the rest of the world's breathing. My subconscious running away was their security. My burning desire to be loved was their ability to calmly attract it.

Now I can see clearly. I made bail. I won the trial and I am not looking back.

New chapters can begin once life's challenges wake us up. Hell did this for me. Hell has been good to me. This was not the case in the moment. The hardest part wasn't being hit; it was being permanently awoken from my lifelong coma and waiting for the dust to settle. It was figuring out how to walk again and how to calm my nervous system every minute of the day after being re-exposed to real time. It was being forced to explore this wild jungle of a world but, this time, alive and with my guard down.

I remind myself to always stay curious. Curiosity didn't kill the cat. Curiosity is the cat. It lives within the cat's soul. Repression and heartbreak is what killed the cat. You cannot take away curiosity; you can only numb the body and mind in which it sits. Thankfully, your soul is not destined or designed to be stuck. It is far too divine to not find escape. Curiosity saved this cat's life.

WE OFTEN CHECK OUT OF A BODY THAT IS TOO PAINFUL TO SIT IN.

---

NOW I HAVE RETURNED, I FEEL NAKED. I FEEL SEEN. EVERYTHING HURTS. I AM TENDER WORRY, AS I WRESTLE WITH THE NEXT TRIAL, TURNING THIS TRIBULATION INTO RESILIENCE. I WILL CONTINUE TO SPEAK THE WORDS INSIDE ME AND RELEASE THE PAIN THROUGH LANGUAGE. EVEN IF IT IS ON PAPER AND ADDRESSED TO ME.

---

Affirmation: I choose to set free my suffering and return.

MY DISSOCIATIVE MENTAL STATE FOOLED YOU INTO THINKING I WASN'T FUCKING BRILLIANT.

---

YOU'VE NEVER KNOWN STABLE ME. WELCOME, AND BEWARE.

---

Affirmation: I choose to show my capabilities. I choose to make change. I choose to leave my mark.

## APPROACH CONTRASTING VIEWS WITH FASCINATION INSTEAD OF RIDICULE.

---

NEGATIVE JUDGEMENT USES TOO MUCH OF OUR BEAUTIFUL ENERGY. REMEMBER: YOU ARE NOT BEING SILENCED WHEN SOMEONE CHALLENGES YOUR BELIEFS. IF IT ISN'T WRAPPED IN DISCRIMINATION OR PREJUDICE, BE INTERESTED.

---

Affirmation: I choose to allow space for other opinions.

IT'S YOUR RESPONSIBILITY TO HELP YOUR TRAUMATISED BRAIN WITH ITS ASSIGNMENT TO RETURN BACK TO REALITY.

---

NO-ONE HAS THE RIGHT TO GET IN THE WAY OF YOUR HEALING. PUSH ASIDE ALL EXPECTATIONS AND MAKE RECOVERY YOUR FULLTIME JOB. LET THEM DOWN. LET THEM ALL DOWN. ESPECIALLY IF IT MEANS YOU WON'T BE LETTING YOURSELF DOWN.

---

Affirmation: I choose to let others down and prioritise my recovery.

## THERE'S ENOUGH SPACE FOR YOU HERE.

---

LET'S ERADICATE THE IDEA THAT WE DO NOT BELONG. WE ALL BELONG. SOME OF US JUST SHINE A LITTLE DIFFERENTLY. THERE IS A TRIBE AWAITING US ALL. IF YOU HAVEN'T FOUND YOURS YET, MAYBE IT'S TIME TO SEARCH IN DIFFERENT ROOMS.

---

Affirmation: I choose to find a tribe suited for me.

## A CHEMICAL IMBALANCE CAN ALIGN WITH CONSISTENT SELF-COMPASSION.

---

TRAUMA REQUIRES A WHOLE LOT OF SELF-LOVE TO HEAL AND REWIRE THE DAMAGE THAT HAS OCCURRED TO THE BRAIN. CATCH YOURSELF IN YOUR NEGATIVE THOUGHTS. CUT THEM OFF AND REPLACE THEM WITH EMPATHY. SHAME AND GUILT CANNOT SURVIVE WHEN EMPATHY IS PRESENT.

---

Affirmation: I choose self-compassion from here on.

YOU'RE PRETTY HARD ON YOURSELF. REMEMBER WE'RE JUST CHEMICALS.

---

TO RELEASE THE GOOD CHEMICALS, TRY THE FOLLOWING: EAT DARK CHOCOLATE, DANCE, SING LOUDLY, TAKE COLD SHOWERS, JOURNAL, BE WITH FRIENDS, WATCH THE COMEDY CHANNEL, BE WELL RESTED, REPEAT.

---

Affirmation: I choose to release good chemicals in my brain.

## THE WORLD WOULDN'T BE BETTER OFF WITHOUT YOU.

---

WHAT IF I PROMISED YOU THAT IT WILL GET BETTER? I LOVE YOU. KEEP GOING. YOU ARE MUCH STRONGER THAN YOU THINK.

---

Lifeline: 131114

---

Affirmation: Today, I choose to stay.

FEAR: FANTASIES
ENVISAGED AS REAL.

---

RUMOUR HAS IT THAT FEAR IS FAKE.

---

Affirmation: I choose not to
entertain negative fantasies.

TRANSMIT YOUR PAIN ONTO OTHERS ALL YOU WANT; IT WILL NOT HEAL IT.

---

IF YOU'RE AWARE YOUR TRAUMA IS HURTING OTHERS AND CHOOSE TO DO NOTHING, YOU HAVE NOW TAKEN ON THE ROLE OF BULLY. KNOWINGLY SPREADING YOUR PAIN IS IRRESPONSIBLE. IT IS TIME TO GET THE HELP YOU NEED.

---

Affirmation: I choose to get help.

## I WISH IT WORKED OUT BETWEEN US.

---

QUICK UPDATE: I AM THRILLED IT DID NOT WORK OUT BETWEEN US. IT ALL HURT TOO MUCH FOR ME TO BELIEVE I WAS READY FOR YOU AT THAT TIME. I DO NOT CHOOSE PEOPLE WHO DO NOT CHOOSE ME. IN MOMENTS OF HEARTBREAK, WE MUST NOT FORGET HOW TRANSFORMATIVE OUR GRIEF IS; HOW IT POINTS US TO THE REAL WOUND AND LEADS THE WAY TO WHAT IS MEANT FOR US.

---

Affirmation: I choose to let my grief cleanse me.

YOU DID THE BEST YOU COULD WITH THE TRAUMA YOU HAD.

---

YOU DON'T HAVE THE RIGHT TO JUDGE YOUR YOUNGER SELF. INSTEAD, GIVE YOURSELF THE SAME KINDNESS AND UNDERSTANDING YOU EFFORTLESSLY HAND OVER TO EVERYONE ELSE.
YOU ARE HUMAN AND THEREFORE WORTHY OF FORGIVENESS.

---

Affirmation: I choose to never judge myself harshly.

IF THIS BOOK GOES OFF, WE ARE GOING TO BORA BORA.

---

STAT.

---

Affirmation: I choose to envision my successes.

FIND COMFORT IN SPARKING THE IDEA THAT THE PAIN WILL ALL MAKE SENSE ONE DAY.

---

OF COURSE IT WILL. TOO MANY HAVE LED BEFORE YOU AND SHOWN YOU HOW IT IS DONE FOR YOU TO THINK OTHERWISE.

---

Affirmation: I choose to believe life-changing growth will come from this journey.

IF SOMEONE'S WEIGHT HAS CHANGED, YOU DON'T NEED TO TELL THEM.

---

CAN WE TAKE THE STIGMA OUT OF THE WORD 'FAT' NOW? FAT IS BEAUTIFUL. FAT IS SEXY. FAT DOES NOT EQUAL BAD. WHAT WE HAVE LEARNED IS BAD. AND HARMFUL. THE SAME GOES FOR THINNER BODIES. YOU ARE ASTOUNDINGLY BEAUTIFUL. ALL SHAPES AND SIZES BELONG. UNLEARN THE BULLSHIT AND START LOVING PEOPLE THE WAY WE WERE DESIGNED TO LOVE – WITHOUT EGO.

---

Affirmation: I choose not to body-shame others or myself.

# THEY'RE NOT EVIL. THEY'RE HURTING.

---

THIS IS A BIG ONE. WHEN SOMEONE HURTS YOU DEEPLY, IT IS SO EASY TO VIEW THEIR DEVIOUSNESS AS A PERSONALITY TRAIT, RATHER THAN AN OVERFLOW OF THEIR OWN PAIN, COMBINED WITH AN INABILITY TO TRANSFORM IT. IF WE DO NOT FORGIVE, WE WILL ALWAYS END UP HURTING BECAUSE WE HAVE CHOSEN TO REMAIN STUCK IN THE SELF-HATRED THEY TAUGHT US.

---

Affirmation: I choose to understand, forgive and move on because I am deserving of peace.

THE MOMENT I CHOSE MYSELF – I MEAN, REALLY DISREGARDED EVERYONE ELSE'S DESIRES FOR ME AND LISTENED TO MY HEART – THAT WAS THE MOMENT I FINALLY FOUND THAT MISSING PUZZLE PIECE.

---

I WILL BE VERY CAREFUL WITH WHAT I DO WITH MY TIME. IF IT DOES NOT ALIGN WITH MY SPIRIT, I WILL SHOW COURAGE AND DISPOSE OF IT.

---

Affirmation: I choose to match today's tasks with my heart's values.

## RAISE YOUR SON TO BELIEVE CRYING IS A NECESSITY.

---

FROM BEGINNING TO END, BOYS AND MEN ARE FED THE DESTRUCTIVE MESSAGE – YOU WILL BE FEMINISED IF YOU FEEL. THIS IS VIOLENT FOR EVERYONE. NEWSFLASH: YOU ARE FEMININE AND MASCULINE. YOU ARE HUMAN. PLEASE CONDITION YOUR SON TO BELIEVE CRYING IS HIS CHANCE FOR CONTINUAL REBIRTH, INSTEAD OF THE PATH TO EMASCULATION. FEELING IS NOT YOUR INTRODUCTION TO FEMININITY. IT IS YOUR INTRODUCTION TO HUMANITY, WHOLENESS AND SELF. PAIN HAS TO COME OUT. IT IS UP TO THE PARENTS TO ENCOURAGE TEARS OR HABITS OF VIOLENCE.

---

Affirmation: I choose to point all men in my life toward vulnerability and health.

CONSENT ONLY COMES IN THE FORM OF LANGUAGE, NOT SILENCE.

---

TO PROCEED IN SUCH DEAFENING SILENCE CONFIRMS YOU ARE NOT REALLY LISTENING. TRULY LISTENING REQUIRES THE BREAKING OF SILENCE.

---

Affirmation: I choose to truly listen.

## FOCUS ON YOUR PHYSIOLOGY. EXAMINE IT.

---

I AM A HAWK. YOU ARE MY PREY. I WILL PROCESS AND DIGEST ALL OF MY BODY'S UNHELPFUL SENSATIONS.

---

Affirmation: I choose to understand my painful reactions.

IT'S 4 AM AND THE DRUGS ARE WEARING OFF. WHAT A SHAME; I STILL DON'T LIKE ME.

---

TRY SHINING LIGHT ON YOUR GRIEF INSTEAD OF NUMBING IT.

---

Affirmation: I choose to overcome the fright I feel about my pain.

HE WIPED HIS OWN TEARS. HE PATTED HIMSELF ON THE BACK. HE FOUGHT TOO MANY SILENT BATTLES AND, ALTHOUGH IT WAS THE MOST UNIMAGINABLE PAIN, HE WOULDN'T HAVE IT ANY OTHER WAY. WHY? BECAUSE HE UNDERSTANDS NOW THAT IT WAS THE ONLY WAY HE'D FIND HIS WAY BACK TO HIMSELF.

---

NO MATTER HOW HORRIFIC THE PAIN, OR THE LENGTH IN WHICH IT HAS PROLONGED, DO NOT TAKE FOR GRANTED THIS WONDERFUL OPPORTUNITY TO DO ALL THE SELF-WORK YOU NEVER KNEW YOU NEEDED. I NEED YOU TO BE REALLY BRAVE NOW. ANNOUNCE YOUR NEW-FOUND RESILIENCE. I PROMISE YOU'RE GETTING BETTER, EVEN WHEN YOU FEEL STUCK. YOU'RE READING THIS SO YOU'RE DOING THE WORK. I AM SO PROUD OF YOU.

---

Affirmation: I choose to unlock the beast that is my resilience.

IF YOU CAN'T CONTROL
YOUR EMOTIONAL PAIN,
YOU MAY SEEK TO CONTROL
SOMEONE ELSE'S.

---

HURT PEOPLE HURT PEOPLE.
I AM THANKFUL THAT HEALED
PEOPLE HEAL PEOPLE.

---

Affirmation: I choose to heal
and then heal others.

LET'S DO A 360 AND SHOW OURSELVES LOVE INSTEAD OF PUNISHMENT.

---

WHEN WILL YOU HAVE SUFFERED ENOUGH? YOU WERE NOT BORN FOR CONTINUOUS TORMENT.

---

Affirmation: I choose to stop punishing myself.

THE ACT OF CHASING A PERSON ONLY HIGHLIGHTS YOUR FIRM BELIEF THAT YOU ARE NOT ENOUGH FOR SOMEONE TO LOVE.

---

YOU ARE ENOUGH FOR SOMEONE TO LOVE. WITHIN THESE BELIEFS, WHAT IS TRULY NEEDED IS MORE LOVE FOR SELF. YOU DON'T NEED TO PROVE ANYTHING TO ANYONE. JUST BE.

---

Affirmation: I choose to chase myself.

## PRACTICE LISTENING TO YOURSELF EVERY DAY.

---

THIS REQUIRES SUCH SKILL; NOT LISTENING TO ALL THE OTHER VOICES AND IDENTIFYING WHICH VOICE WITHIN YOU ISN'T AN IMPOSTER DRIVEN BY EXPECTATION OR ANXIETY. THE BEST ADVICE I CAN GIVE YOU IS TO DISTANCE YOURSELF FROM UNHELPFUL PEOPLE AND NOISE. SIT IN SILENCE. THINK ABOUT SOMETHING THAT IS WEIGHING HEAVILY ON YOU. REPEAT: I CHOOSE TO LISTEN TO MYSELF. IF YOU HAVE EVEN A MOMENT OF DIVINITY OR INNER-KNOWING PASS OVER YOU, YOU'LL KNOW WHAT IS TRUTHFUL AND WHAT IS NOT.

---

Affirmation: I choose to actively listen to myself.

GASLIGHT ME TO THE POINT OF INSANITY AND I'LL SHOW YOU EXACTLY WHAT SELF-LOVE LOOKS LIKE.

---

I AM UNINTERESTED, UNAMUSED AND UNBOTHERED BY YOU. I WILL PICK UP THE PIECES WITH A GENTLE SMILE, AND REMAIN HOPEFUL, EAGER AND FAR TOO FOCUSED ON MY COMEBACK TO ACKNOWLEDGE YOU. MY SMILE IS SO KIND, SO PURE AND SO SOFT. I DIDN'T LOSE IT. IT MAKES YOU QUESTION YOUR OWN WORTH AND RESILIENCE. YOU'VE NOW BEEN FORCED TO REALISE THE PROBLEM WAS ALWAYS YOU.

---

Affirmation: I choose not to hand over my power.

YOU CANNOT LOVE SOMEBODY PROPERLY UNTIL YOU LOVE YOURSELF PROPERLY.

---

CHOOSE ME, THEN WE CAN CHOOSE THEM. (INNER CHILD)

I WANT YOU TO PRACTICE WRITING THREE THINGS YOU LOVE ABOUT YOURSELF EVERY DAY. THEN, I WANT YOU TO WATCH YOUR LIFE CHANGE.

---

Affirmation: I choose me first.

YOU'RE SUFFERING IN YOUR RELATIONSHIP BECAUSE YOU'RE NOT LISTENING TO YOURSELF.

---

THAT LITTLE VOICE MAKES A BIG POINT. IT'S TIME TO ACKNOWLEDGE IT AND ACT.

---

Affirmation: I choose to reflect on my truth and make change accordingly.

I AM UNAPOLOGETICALLY ME. NOT IN A NASTY WAY. MY SPIRIT IS ALIGNED AND SECURE.

---

NO NEED TO PLEASE. NO NEED TO FLAUNT. I AM GLORIOUS AND HAVE SUCCEEDED IN ALL THINGS TRUTHFUL.

---

Affirmation: I choose to feed my secure self.

LOVE EVERY PART OF THEM THAT SEES YOU AS A THREAT.

---

YOUR SECURITY MAKES SOME FEEL THREATENED. PLEASE, TEACH THEM THE TYPE OF KINDNESS THEY'RE CRAVING FROM THEMSELVES.

---

Affirmation: I choose not to be negatively affected by people who are hurting but to demonstrate love in spite of their behaviour.

CONTINUE TO HEAL THE HIDDEN PARTS OF YOURSELF UNTIL YOU FIND THE COURAGE TO SET THEM FREE INTO THE WORLD.

---

SET IT ALL FREE AT YOUR OWN PACE. THE MOST TRANSFORMATIVE TIME OF YOUR LIFE WAS NEVER GOING TO BE A QUICK JOURNEY.

---

Affirmation: I choose to surrender to pressure and timelines.

DO NOT GIVE SOMEBODY ELSE THE RESPONSIBILITY OF YOUR HEALING FOR THEY WILL NOT BE ABLE TO COMPLETE THIS MISSION FULLY.

---

IF I COULD KISS YOUR HEART, I WOULD. HOWEVER, HEALING A HEART IS A SUPERPOWER POSSESSED ONLY WITHIN THE INDIVIDUAL.

---

Affirmation: I choose to be my own hero.

IF SOMEONE IS HURTING,
IT ISN'T YOUR JOB TO SAY,
"NO, YOU'RE NOT." IT IS YOUR
JOB TO SAY, "HOW CAN I HELP?"

---

YOU MAY NOT GET IT. HOWEVER,
'GETTING IT' IS IRRELEVANT
WHEN SOMEONE IS IN PAIN.

---

Affirmation: I choose to stand alongside hurt people and minorities with compassion.

DANCE, DANCE, DANCE.
DANCE IN THE FUCKED-UP
SPACE THAT IS UNCERTAINTY.

---

THAT'S WHERE ALL THE GOOD
SHIT HAPPENS, BABY.

---

Affirmation: I choose to expand
and mature in my discomfort.

LEAN INTO YOUR GRIEF.
IT CAN CLEANSE YOU IN
WONDERFUL WAYS.

---

CRY OUT LOUD. CRY PROUDLY. CRY WHILE
LISTENING TO ADELE ON REPEAT.

---

Affirmation: I choose to cleanse myself.

A TRAUMATIC EVENT IS
AN OPPORTUNITY TO
REINVENT YOURSELF.

---

REWIRING YOUR BRAIN BACK TO SANITY AFTER BEING DEEPLY TRAUMATISED IS YOUR CHANCE TO TRANSFORM YOUR BELIEF SYSTEM AND LIFE. THE SLATE HAS JUST BEEN WIPED CLEAN. THIS IS YOUR FRESH START.

---

Affirmation: I choose to create beauty through pain.

TODAY WILL BE A GREAT DAY.

---

REPEAT DAILY.

---

Affirmation: I choose to set myself up for a beautiful day.

## ACCEPTANCE > CONTROL.

---

SURRENDER AND SAVE YOUR
ENERGY WHERE YOU CAN.

---

Affirmation: I choose to surrender to life's flow.

NO-ONE WILL KNOW
THE VIOLENCE IT TOOK TO
BECOME THIS GENTLE.

---

IF YOU HAVE LET YOUR CRUEL
TREATMENT LEAD YOU TO AN EVEN
MORE BENIGN VERSION OF YOURSELF,
YOU, MY DEAR, ARE A SUPERHERO.

---

Affirmation: I choose to be soft,
tender and affectionate.

WHEN NOTHING IS CERTAIN, YOU ABSOLUTELY HAVE THE CHOICE TO FOCUS ON WHAT YOU DO WANT TO HAPPEN.

---

DON'T UNDERESTIMATE THE POWER OF YOUR BRAIN. START MANIFESTING AND SEEING YOURSELF DOING THE WORK TO ACHIEVE YOUR GOALS AND DESIRES. A POSITIVE MIND WILL SHIFT ALL OUTCOMES IN YOUR LIFE.

---

Affirmation: I choose to manifest the hard work that comes before achievement.

AND THEN I DECIDED TO
STOP FEEDING THE FEAR.

---

BECAUSE I REALISED THIS IS A DECISION
I HAVE FULL CONTROL OVER.

---

Affirmation: I choose to believe
in what will benefit me.

BE THE ARTIST OF
YOUR UNIVERSE.

---

I WILL SCULPT THE MIND I DESERVE
AND, THUS, THE LIFE I DREAM OF.

---

Affirmation: I choose to design
a masterpiece of a life.

TRUE LOVE WILL NEVER BE COUNTERACTED WITH SUFFERING.

---

IT IS NEVER TOO LATE TO BE THE LOVE OF YOUR LIFE. LEAVE WHAT IS HURTING YOU AND RUN TOWARD YOURSELF AGAIN.

---

Affirmation: I choose to do what will set me free.

## I FIND MYSELF CLASHING WITH OLD BELIEFS THAT NO LONGER SERVE ME.

---

I AM STILL UNLEARNING AND I AM LOVING IT. THERE IS NO RUSH. I KNOW IT IS IMPOSSIBLE FOR THERE TO BE A WINNER AS THIS RACE HAS NO FINISH LINE. I JUST KEEP ON SMILING WIDER AND WIDER EACH DAY AS I BECOME A MORE TRUTHFUL VERSION OF MYSELF. FREEDOM FEELS SO HOLY.

---

Affirmation: I choose to enjoy my journey to peace, emotional stability and good health.

THIS AÇAI BOWL IS
INCREDIBLY BLAND.

---

HOW BLESSED I AM TO HAVE FOOD.

---

Affirmation: I choose gratitude
over a lack of appreciation.

SCIENCE HAS PROVEN THAT IF YOU RETURN FOOD AT A RESTAURANT, YOU'RE PROBABLY A DICKHEAD.

---

I'VE NEVER UNDERSTOOD THIS. EAT THE FOOD, BABE. PEOPLE ARE LITERALLY STARVING TO DEATH AND YOU'RE FUSSING BECAUSE YOUR LOBSTER IS ROOM TEMP.

---

Affirmation: I choose not to be a fuck-face.

IF FEAR IS YOUR ENERGETIC, YOU'LL BE ARRIVING AT EVERYONE'S DOOR WITH THE CHALLENGE OF NEEDING TO BE SAVED.

---

IF THIS RESONATED WITH YOU, WAKE UP EACH MORNING AND SAY THE FOLLOWING AFFIRMATIONS.

---

Affirmations: I choose to release my fears. I choose to question my limiting self-beliefs. I choose to save myself. I choose to believe my true self is enough.

HARM TAKES PLACE WHEN WE CHOOSE TO WATER WEEDS.

---

CATASTROPHISED OR INTRUSIVE THOUGHTS ARE REALLY JUST WEEDS. STOP GIVING THEM SO MUCH POWER.

---

Affirmation: I choose to water my ideal outcomes.

## A CONCRETE BELIEF CAN CRUMBLE WITH COUNTERACTIVE AFFIRMATIVE LANGUAGE.

---

IF YOU HAVE A BELIEF THAT IS UNHELPFUL, OR IS SUPPRESSIVE AND THEREFORE MAKING YOU UNWELL, DIG DEEP AND FIND THE KNOWING WITHIN YOU THAT WANTS TO CHALLENGE IT.

---

Affirmation: I choose to challenge harmful beliefs.

DISMANTLING UNHELPFUL BELIEFS CREATES SPACE FOR SELF-LOVE TO ARRIVE.

---

IF YOUR ROOM IS TAKEN UP BY NEGATIVE ENERGY, IT WON'T BE OVERLY INVITING FOR THE THOUGHTS AND PEOPLE YOU'D LOVE TO HAVE ENTER.

---

Affirmation: I choose to clear my mind of negativity in order for joyous things to take its place.

SOMETIMES, IT DOESN'T MATTER IF YOU BELIEVE YOUR REACTIVITY COMES FROM A WELL-INTENTIONED PLACE. IT MATTERS HOW MUCH YOU UNDERSTAND THE ROOT PAIN THAT IS ITS TURBULENCE.

---

YOU WERE NOT ASSIGNED THE JOB OF FEAR-SPREADER. YOU WERE, HOWEVER, GIVEN THE CHOICE TO UNDERSTAND YOUR FEAR'S REASONING.

---

Affirmation: I choose not to spread my fear but, instead, to recognise and dissect it.

SHAME IS A DISEASE THAT
KILLS MOST PEOPLE.

---

LEARN TO LET GO OF YOUR SHAME. YOU DID THE BEST YOU COULD. YOU TRIED AND IT WAS ENOUGH.
NO-ONE IS JUDGING YOU AS HARSHLY AS YOU ARE JUDGING YOURSELF.

---

Affirmation: I choose to release shame.

DON'T ALLOW YOUR FEARS TO HAUNT YOU FOR A SECOND LONGER.

---

YOU DRIVE YOUR LIFE AND YOU ARE IN CONTROL. PERIOD.

---

Affirmation: I choose to believe blessings are always around the corner.

## HAS THE WORST REALLY HAPPENED OR IS THE WORST JUST IN YOUR MIND?

---

WE PUT OURSELVES THROUGH SO MUCH SUFFERING, THOUGH NINETY-NINE PER CENT OF IT IS JUST MISPLACED FEAR. WE NEED TO START BEING REALISTIC WITH OUR INTRUSIVE THOUGHTS AND GIVE OUR ATTENTION TO WHAT IS ACTUALLY BEING PRESENTED IN FRONT OF US. IF A THOUGHT IS WRAPPED IN FEAR AND ANXIETY, IT IS INTRUSIVE AND UNTRUTHFUL. IF IT IS CALM AND PEACEFUL, IT IS INTUITION.

---

Affirmation: Today, I choose to be realistic.

INHALE FOR FOUR. HOLD FOR FOUR. EXHALE FOR FOUR. HOLD FOR FOUR. REPEAT.

---

BOX-BREATHING IS A GENTLE REMINDER TO THE NERVOUS SYSTEM THAT EVERYTHING IS OKAY.

---

Affirmation: I choose to breathe.

# ENOUGH IS ENOUGH AND SO ARE YOU

We have the sun. We have working legs.
We say we deserve more. We tell ourselves we need more.
We have our friends. We laugh so hard.
We gossip about those we love the most. We need them to survive.
We are sometimes mean.
We cry really hard.
We know we should do better.
We are incredibly thoughtful.
We are messy. We are strange. We are funny sometimes.
We are hurt.
We send up our sins.
We smile at strangers.
We fight for love.
We struggle to love ourselves.
We learn to love ourselves a little more.
We fall. We pick ourselves up. We fall even harder. We pray for strength to get back up. We get back up. We fall again.
We pray. We hear nothing. We pray. We hear nothing.
We question our beliefs. We think we hear something. We hope it is all real. We logically do not understand.
We receive answered prayers. We vow to never question again.
We question again.
We fall further.
We stress.

We question everything we have learned.
We stress more.
We realise stress didn't help. We try to stop our stress.
We cry. We heal a bit. We numb a lot.
We suppress.
We suppress.
We suppress.
We believe this is living. We believe this is our sacrifice for worthiness.
We've lost ourselves. We feel nothing.
We feel pain.
We notice what we cannot control. We search for things we can control. We try to control everything. We lose control. We are out of control. We try to control others.
We need more.
We struggle. We give up. We crash. We hit rock bottom.
We realise we hate ourselves.
We learn what to unlearn. We learn to love ourselves again.
We keep self-regulating.
We surrender to life. We no longer fear falling.
We realise we can have it all.
We are free.
We are the divinity.
We aren't looking back.

MY VIBRANCE HAS HELD UP A MIRROR TO YOU AND YOU DON'T LIKE WHAT YOU SEE.

---

TO THE DEFLECTOR: TAKE THIS OPPORTUNITY TO EVOLVE. DO NOT HAVE PRIDE. YOU ARE NOT ANGRY AT THEM; YOU'RE ANGRY AT YOURSELF. YOU ARE NOT THEIR CREATION. YOU BELONG TO YOU. THEY HAVE SIMPLY GIVEN YOU THE GIFT OF AWARENESS. NOW, ACT.

TO THE REFLECTOR: GLOW, EVEN IF IT FORCES THEM TO REASSESS THEIR OWN CONTENTMENT. YOU ARE DOING THE BEST KIND OF WORK – YOU ARE ENCOURAGING CHANGE.

---

Affirmation: I choose to be influenced positively and let my vibrance radiate onto others.

I THINK IT IS IMPORTANT WE ALL SUFFER GREATLY AT LEAST ONCE IN OUR LIVES.

---

SOMETIMES, IT NEEDS TO GET REALLY DARK FOR CHANGE TO OCCUR. IT WILL FORCE US TO BE PROACTIVE IN FINDING OURSELVES AGAIN. I HOPE WE ALL EVENTUALLY LIVE THE LIFE WE WERE DESTINED TO LIVE; ONE WHERE LISTENING TO OURSELVES IS NOT ONLY ENCOURAGED, BUT CELEBRATED.

---

Affirmation: I choose to let negative experiences lead to positive growth and knowing.

BALANCE. WE NEED BALANCE.

---

CREATING TIME FOR REST, WORK, PLAY, LOVE AND SELF ARE SO IMPORTANT IN MAINTAINING YOUR EMOTIONAL HEALTH. THE GRIND IS OVER.

---

Affirmation: I choose balance
in all areas of my life.

# I HOPE YOU NEVER LOSE YOUR CURIOSITY.

---

MAYBE NOTHING WAS MEANT TO BE CERTAIN. MAYBE YOU WEREN'T MEANT TO BE SURE. MAYBE THERE IS BEAUTY IN THAT. CONTINUE TO GET CURIOUS ABOUT YOUR LIFE AND WHAT FEELS AUTHENTIC TO YOU. NEVER LIVE A LIFE WHERE YOU ARE STUCK OR RESTRICTED TO ONE SET OF BELIEFS. NEVER LIVE WITHOUT CHOICE OR INTRIGUE.

---

Affirmation: I choose to get curious.

NARCOTICS ARE THE ONLY WAY YOU CURRENTLY KNOW HOW TO HURT A LITTLE LESS.

---

THE FIRST STEP IS FINDING OUT WHAT YOU'RE NUMBING THEN RUN TOWARD IT.

---

Affirmation: I choose to run toward the answers.

I AM THE RICHEST MAN
I KNOW, EVEN WHEN MY
CARD IS DECLINED.

---

I'VE DONE THE WORK.
MY CORE IS A BILLIONAIRE.

---

Affirmation: I choose to be the best kind of rich – real and restored.

## I AM A NEWBORN WOBBLING MY WAY THROUGH THE UNCERTAINTY WITH EXCITEMENT AND TRUTH.

---

REMEMBER WHEN YOU WERE A KID AND YOU JUST WERE? YOU ROCKED UP TO EVERY HURDLE, FULLY YOURSELF. A NASTY FALL RESULTED IN EITHER CRYING HYSTERICALLY OR LAUGHING HYSTERICALLY. THAT MINOR MOMENT, JUST AFTER THE FALL AND JUST PRIOR TO THE REACTION, WAS UNCERTAIN – BUT IT WAS YOURS. WHATEVER THE OUTCOME, IT WAS REAL AND CATHARTIC. LET'S GET BACK TO THAT PLACE.

---

Affirmation: I choose to wobble through life with a smile and my guard down.

## DON'T INHALE THE WORLD'S OXYGEN JUST TO EXHALE YOUR BAD BREATH.

---

EACH BREATH IS A GIFT AND EACH EXHALE IS AN OPPORTUNITY TO MAKE THIS WORLD A KINDER PLACE. DO NOT JUST TAKE. INSTEAD, SHOW THANKS BY BEING MORE MINDFUL WITH WHAT YOU PRONOUNCE TO THE WORLD.

---

Affirmation: I choose to exhale mindfully and inspiringly.

## CHANGE ‘MY ANXIETY’ TO ‘MY EXCITEMENT’.

---

ANXIETY AND EXCITEMENT USE VERY SIMILAR CHEMICALS IN THE BRAIN. THIS TRICKING THING CAN GO BOTH WAYS, BRAIN.

---

Affirmation: I choose lighter language.

BE SO STRONG THAT YOU ABSOLUTELY REFUSE TO GIVE ANY POWER TO INTRUSIVE THOUGHTS.

---

A THOUGHT CANNOT HARM YOU. IT WILL NOT HARM YOU. WHAT HARMS YOU IS THE RUMINATING, WHICH IS IN YOUR CONTROL.

---

Affirmation: I choose to catch my rumination and cut it off.

THEY'RE GONE. THEY'RE ON TO THE NEXT ONE. THEY AREN'T COMING BACK. TRUTHFULLY, THEY DON'T EVEN THINK ABOUT YOU.

---

I AM TOO TIRED TO BE SCARED OF YOU SO I WON'T BE. IT IS OVER NOW. IT WAS OVER A LONG TIME AGO, ACTUALLY. I JUST HAD TO BELIEVE IT.

YOU CAN SPEND YOUR LIFE HIDING IN FEAR OR YOU CAN CHOOSE TO SAY, "FUCK IT" AND LIVE IN SPITE OF. THAT IS THE TRUTH. PRACTICE THIS MINDSET DAILY. I PROMISE THE ANXIETY WON'T STICK AROUND. YOUR LIFE IS TOO PRECIOUS TO BE CONTROLLED. YOUR MIND IS TOO BEAUTIFUL TO BE TAINTED. WE WILL NOT WASTE ANOTHER SECOND ON ABUSIVE PEOPLE.

---

Affirmation: I choose to let go of the panic and practice fearlessness.

THE COAST IS CLEAR. IT'S SAFE TO COME OUT OF HIDING.

---

SEVERE ANXIETY AND STRESS CAN PLAY VERY REAL TRICKS ON OUR MINDS. YOU ARE SAFE. WALK AROUND THE EGGSHELLS. IT IS OVER.

---

Affirmation: I choose to be logical again.

## WRITE DOWN ALL YOUR INTRUSIVE THOUGHTS AND LAUGH AT HOW SILLY THEY ARE.

---

I KNOW THE DESPERATION OF TRYING TO GET RID OF THOUGHTS THAT HAVE SOMEHOW STUCK TO THE MOST DELICATE PART OF YOUR BRAIN LIKE SUPERGLUE. I NEED YOU TO BE BRAVER THAN EVER IN THIS MOMENT AND LAUGH AT THOSE PETRIFYING THOUGHTS. DISTANCE YOURSELF FROM THEM. IT IS AN EFFECTIVE WAY TO GAIN BACK THE POWER THAT IS RIGHTFULLY YOURS. THIS SKILL AND EYE MOVEMENT DESENSITISATION AND REPROCESSING (EMDR) THERAPY HELPED TO FINALLY SET ME FREE.

---

Affirmation: I choose to take back my power.

WHILE YOU WERE ABUSING ME, I WAS PRAYING FOR YOU.

---

I AM SOFT, DELICATE AND A FORCE OF UNMEASURABLE POWER. I REFUSE TO LET YOU TAKE MY GENTLENESS AWAY FROM ME.

---

Affirmation: I choose to let my sensitivity marry my strength, marry my compassion.

## GOD IS OFFENDED AT THE THOUGHT OF YOU BELIEVING HE IS SO JUDGMENTAL.

---

IMAGINE IF WE VIEWED OUR GOD AS SOMEONE WHO STOOD UP FOR MINORITIES AND DEFENDED THOSE DISOWNED AND REJECTED BY SOCIETY. IMAGINE IF WE VIEWED GOD HOW HE TRULY WAS – SOMEONE WITH ENDLESS COMPASSION AND LOVE FOR US.

---

Affirmation: I choose to believe God is light and soft.

YOU'LL BE JUDGED ON THE PEOPLE YOU HELP, NOT THE MISTAKES YOU MAKE.

---

GOD HAS NO DESIRE TO STRIP YOU OF YOUR HUMANITY OR SEARCH YOU LIKE INTERNET HISTORY. HE IS NOT INTERESTED IN THE GLITCH IN THE SYSTEM THAT IS YOUR LIFE. HE WILL SIMPLY FOCUS ON THE KIND THINGS YOU SAID TO PEOPLE WHO WERE HURTING.

---

Affirmation: I choose to always be loving like God.

IN LIFE, THERE ARE CATS AND DOGS. CATS WILL GO WHERE THEY ARE FED AND AMUSED. DOGS WILL REMAIN OUT OF LOYALTY.

---

DO NOT AMUSE THE CATS AROUND YOU. THE PEOPLE YOU CHOOSE TO KEEP IN YOUR LIFE ARE A REFLECTION OF YOU.

---

Affirmation: I choose to keep loyalty around.

## ARE WE GOING TO TALK ABOUT HOW BEING TRAUMATISED FEELS LIKE A REPEATED DAY ONE OF SOBRIETY?

---

BEING TRAUMATISED FEELS LIKE SCULLING ICED WATER AND GETTING THAT TOOTH FREEZE ON YOUR FRONT TWO TEETH; EXCEPT, IT'S NOT FOR A FEW SECONDS. IT'S ALL DAY, EVERY DAY. IT FEELS LIKE NAILS ON A CHALKBOARD, EXCEPT IT'S ALL DAY, EVERY DAY. IT FEELS LIKE SOMEONE HAS TAKEN AWAY ALL YOUR SKIN AND YOU ARE BARE AND INCREDIBLY SENSITIVE. ALL DAY. EVERY. DAY. EVERYTHING HURTS A MILLION TIMES MORE. WORDS HIT YOU LIKE THEY NEVER HAVE. ABUSIVE BEHAVIOUR FROM OTHERS IS CLEARER THAN EVER. WHAT MAKES BEING TRAUMATISED SO BEAUTIFUL IS HOW THE INDIVIDUAL DISCOVERS THEIR COURAGE TO WALK AWAY FROM EVERY SINGLE THING THAT HELPED PUT THEM IN THAT STATE.

---

Affirmation: I choose to use my trauma as a weapon to make change.

## HERE'S TO THE FRIENDS WHO CRY WHEN WE SUCCEED OR FAIL.

---

A DEDICATION:

I ADORE MY FRIENDS. I LOVE EACH AND EVERY ONE OF YOU. YOU ARE MY CHOSEN FAMILY, THE LOVES OF MY LIFE. YOU ARE MY PEOPLE. YOU KNOW WHO YOU ARE. YOUR SUPPORT SAVES ME EVERY DAY. I WILL NEVER FORGET. THANK YOU FOR CHOOSING ME. I WILL ALWAYS CHOOSE YOU.

---

Affirmation: I choose to keep our love alive.

IF YOU'RE DRAINED AFTER YOU LEAVE THEM, IT MAY BE TIME TO REASSESS THE RELATIONSHIP.

---

I AM TIRED OF YOU ROBBING ME OF MY PRECIOUS ENERGY. I AM AN EMPATH BUT I REFUSE TO LET PEOPLE PULL ME AWAY FROM MYSELF ANYMORE.

---

Affirmation: I choose to prioritise my wellbeing.

REJECTION IS MOST PAINFUL WHEN IT COMES FROM ONESELF.

---

I WILL NEVER AGAIN REJECT MY OWN HEART. REJECTING MY HEART IS DISPOSING OF THE MOST TRUTHFUL PART OF MYSELF. I AM FOREVER A TRUTH-SEEKER. I CANNOT LIE ANYMORE.

---

Affirmation: I choose to no longer shun myself for others.

STAYING SILENT MEANS YOU AGREE.

---

BE AWARE OF THE CONVERSATIONS YOU DON'T SPEAK UP ON. NOTHING EVER CHANGED WITHOUT DISCOMFORT.

---

Affirmation: I choose to speak up when something doesn't sit right with me.

IN A WORLD WHERE SELF-ABANDONMENT IS ENTRAPMENT FOR THE MAJORITY, I CHOOSE TO LISTEN TO THAT LITTLE VOICE WE ARE TAUGHT TO SILENCE.

---

PLEASE STOP IGNORING YOUR DEEPEST DESIRES. YOUR PREFERRED PATH IS ALWAYS GOING TO LEAD TO JOY, TRUTH, DESTINY AND THE UNLOCKING OF SELF.

---

Affirmation: I choose to quieten the voices around me and reverberate the little voice within me that tells me what I need to thrive.

UNTIL YOU ARE EMOTIONALLY STABLE, YOU WILL ALWAYS ATTRACT A LOVER WHO WILL SHOW YOU EXACTLY WHERE YOU ARE STILL CAGED.

---

I GUARANTEE, IF YOU LOOK CLOSELY ENOUGH AT ALL YOUR EX-PARTNERS, THEY WILL HIGHLIGHT THE ROOM IN YOUR INNER HOME THAT IS EITHER LOCKED, ABANDONED OR BEEN VANDALISED. BE VERY AWARE OF WHAT YOU ARE ATTRACTING. THEY ARE PROVIDING YOU WITH THE STEPPING STONES TO WHERE YOU ARE STILL HELD CAPTIVE.

---

Affirmation: I choose to pay attention to what I attract and let it guide me to freedom.

SO MANY MELODIES MISSED WHILE TRYING TO FIND THE HARMONY LINE.

---

CHILDREN LAUGHING. DOGS HEAVILY PANTING. OCEAN WAVES. WIND SHACKLING THE PALM TREES. LIFE'S MELODIES ARE A GIFT. REMEMBER TO LISTEN OUT FOR THEM.

---

Affirmation: I choose to keep my ears open to life's beautiful melodies.

## ENTERING THE FLOW STATE IS HOW YOU GET RID OF MENTAL PAIN.

---

YOU NEED TO RE-ENTER PRESENT TIME.

THE FLOW STATE: A STATE WHERE YOU ARE TOO PREOCCUPIED TRYING TO ACHIEVE A TASK, YOUR MIND IS PHYSICALLY UNABLE TO FOCUS ON ITS TROUBLES. HOWEVER YOU CHOOSE TO ENTER, MAKE SURE THE TASK AT HAND IS BOTH CHALLENGING AND ACHIEVABLE.

SUGGESTIONS FOR ENTERING THE FLOW STATE: ROCK CLIMBING OR BOULDERING, COLD SHOWERS, ICE BATHS, SWIM IN THE OCEAN, DANCE CLASSES, KNEEL NEXT TO YOUR BED, HANDS IN THE AIR AND YELL, PRAYER, WORK PROJECTS, MASSAGES, EXERCISE, MUSIC (SINGING LOUDLY), COMEDY TV.

---

Affirmation: I choose to enter present time through The Flow State.

## ST MICHAEL THE ARCHANGEL – SAINT OF PROTECTION

---

ST MICHAEL THE ARCHANGEL, DEFEND US IN BATTLE, BE OUR PROTECTION AGAINST THE WICKEDNESS AND SNARES OF THE DEVIL. MAY GOD REBUKE HIM WE HUMBLY PRAY; AND DO THOU, O PRINCE OF THE HEAVENLY HOST, BY THE POWER OF GOD, CAST INTO HELL SATAN AND ALL THE EVIL SPIRITS WHO PROWL ABOUT THE WORLD SEEKING THE RUIN OF SOULS.

AMEN.

ST MICHAEL, PROTECT ME FROM HARM AND MAKE ME FEEL SAFE AGAIN.

---

Affirmation: I choose to believe in answered prayers.

I HAVE MASTERED THE ART OF MAKING OTHERS FEEL SAFE BECAUSE I HAVE FELT SO INCREDIBLY UNSAFE.

---

CHEEKY BRAIN TRICKED ME INTO THINKING MY WORLD WAS OVER. UPDATE: IT'S NOT AND NEITHER IS YOURS. I PROMISE YOU'LL SEE IT SOON.

---

Affirmation: I choose to be a source of safety for all those who cross my path.

## CHOOSE TO BE REALISTIC AGAIN.

---

HELLO. HI. IT'S ME. THE REALIST IN YOU. YOU HAVE IGNORED ME FOR SO LONG. FANTASY IS MY IMITATOR AND I THINK IT'S TIME WE DITCH HIM.

---

Affirmation: I choose to take back ownership of my mind.

EACH DAY I SIT. I SIT IN STILLNESS; EMOTIONS SCREAMING, INNER CHILD CRYING, INNER WORLD COLLAPSING, HEAD THROBBING, HEART RACING, HOT. I LOOK OUT THE WINDOW AND I WONDER MANY THINGS.

---

07/04/21

I WONDER HOW MUCH LONGER I'LL NEED TO SIT IN THIS PAIN UNTIL I BECOME BIGGER THAN IT. I WONDER WHEN THIS TEST WILL END. I WONDER WHEN IT WON'T BE MY TURN ANYMORE. I WONDER HOW PEOPLE GET THROUGH A MENTAL HEALTH CRISIS. I WONDER IF I'LL EVER FEEL LIKE ME AGAIN. IT SADDENS ME THAT I NOW HAVE A DEEP UNDERSTANDING AS TO WHY PEOPLE CHECK OUT.

03/05/22

I PRAYED FOR LOVE TO BE MY SAVIOUR FOR YEARS. NOW I CAN SEE; I DID NOT REQUIRE ANOTHER TO SAVE ME. TRUTHFULLY, IT WAS MY JOB. A JOB I STRAYED FROM. A JOB WHOSE IMPORTANCE I MISUNDERSTOOD. A JOB IN WHICH I WAS MISGUIDED. A JOB THAT PAIN LED ME BACK TO. A JOB I MANAGED MESSILY. I STUMBLED AND FELL BUT IT WAS MY ACCOMPLISHMENT ALONE. NOW, LOVE FOR SELF HAS ALLOWED ME TO REST.

---

Affirmation: I choose to acknowledge my feelings and my progress, and to not let bad days define me.

REPLACE 'I DON'T WANT [THIS] TO HAPPEN' WITH 'I WANT [THIS] TO HAPPEN'.

---

FOCUSING ON WHAT YOU DO WANT WILL ATTRACT EXACTLY THAT. FOR EXAMPLE, I DO WANT A SEXY, WELL-DRESSED DOCTOR TO FIND ME.

---

Affirmation: I choose to shift my focus.

A PARENT'S JOB: "EVERYTHING IS GOING TO BE ABSOLUTELY FINE. I WILL ALWAYS KEEP YOU SAFE. YOU DON'T NEED TO WORRY ABOUT A THING."

---

*CHILD EXITS THE HOME.
THE PARENT'S WORLD FALLS APART.*

THE MOST CRUCIAL JOB A PARENT HAS IS TO ACT CALM WHEN THEY ARE NOT. THIS IS THE LIFELONG ROLE YOU'RE CONTRACTED TO. IT IS YOUR JOB TO FIGURE OUT HOW TO SHOW UP FOR YOUR CHILD IN THE WAY *THEY* NEED. PLEASE LISTEN TO YOUR CHILDREN, ESPECIALLY WHEN THEY ARE IN CRISIS MODE. THAT IS YOUR SIGNATURE, ISN'T IT?

---

Affirmation: I choose, as a parent, to be a superhero for my child.

YOU'RE KIND AND YOU'RE SMART. THAT'S REALLY AS GOOD AS IT GETS.

---

YOU DO NOT NEED TO GO ABOVE AND BEYOND TO BE ENOUGH. YOU WERE BORN ENOUGH AND NO MATTER WHAT IS TROUBLING YOUR MIND, YOU WILL ALWAYS BE ENOUGH. THAT MUCH IS NOT UP TO YOU. BREATHING MAKES YOU INHERENTLY DESERVING.

---

Affirmation: I choose to let go of the idea that I need to work tirelessly for enough-ness.

## DISSOCIATION IS THE MIND TRYING TO SAVE US FROM THREAT.

---

IF YOU ARE SOMEONE WHO IS CONSTANTLY LEAVING THEIR BODY WHEN STRESSED, IT IS IMPORTANT TO DIFFERENTIATE BETWEEN WHEN YOU TRULY ARE IN DANGER AND WHEN YOUR FEAR RESPONSE HAS BEEN TRIGGERED FOR NO LOGICAL REASON. REMEMBER: WE ARE WIRED TO FOCUS ON THE NEGATIVE. THIS GOES BACK TO PRIMITIVE TIMES. IF THERE WAS MOVEMENT IN THE BUSHES, IT WAS A LION. THIS ANXIETY WAS A SURVIVAL MECHANISM. IT IS RARELY HELPFUL IN THIS DAY AND AGE. THE FOLLOWING WILL HELP YOU QUIETEN THIS NEGATIVE BIAS: A THERAPIST, BREATH WORK, SELF-HELP BOOKS, A CLEAN DIET, BALANCE, THE SUPPORT OF LOVED ONES, GETTING OFF TECHNOLOGY AND INTO NATURE.

---

Affirmation: I choose health and stability for myself.

WHEN BEING WHAT YOU WANT, I ATTRACT CLOWNS. WHEN BEING WHAT I WANT, I ATTRACT SOME GOOD TIMES. WHEN BEING WHO I AM, I ATTRACT ALL THAT BELONGS TO ME.

---

I WILL NO LONGER SHOW UP AS MY FAKE SELF OR APOLOGISE FOR MY EXISTENCE. WE WILL NO LONGER BE NEGOTIATING MY IDENTITY. PERIOD.

---

Affirmation: I choose to live my life without hesitation. I choose to do the right thing and live my truth. I choose to reject abuse. I choose boundaries. I choose to be full of self.

## FROM WANTING TO DIE TO LEARNING TO THRIVE, YOU'VE COME A LONG WAY.

---

A MENTAL HEALTH CRISIS – AKA, WHEN EVERY LITTLE NEGATIVE PIECE OF YOU COMES FLOODING OUT – CAN REALLY MESS WITH YOUR SENSE OF ACCOMPLISHMENT. PLEASE KNOW THIS: YOU HAVE WORKED TIRELESSLY TO COME AS FAR AS YOU HAVE. YOU ARE ASTOUNDING TO STILL BE STANDING. YOUR SUCCESS STORY IS BRILLIANT AND YOUR ACHIEVEMENTS ARE GROUNDBREAKING. NO-ONE, AND I MEAN NO-ONE, HAS THE POWER TO TAKE AWAY THE COURAGE YOU PAINSTAKINGLY SEARCHED FOR TO MAKE IT THIS FAR. YOU ARE A SURVIVOR. NEVER FORGET THAT.

---

Affirmation: I choose, for just three minutes, to acknowledge how far I have come.

## FOR THOSE REALLY TOUGH, ANXIOUS DAYS:

---

HAVE A CHEESE TOASTIE (CARBS, FAT, PROTEIN), DRINK AN ORANGE JUICE (SUGAR), SPRINT OUTSIDE OR ON THE SPOT FOR FIVE TO TEN MINUTES (RELEASE THE ANXIOUS ENERGY), DO FOUR SETS OF EIGHT PUSHUPS (IF STRUGGLING, YOU CAN BALANCE ON YOUR KNEES), GET A HEAD MASSAGE OR WASH YOUR HAIR IN THE SHOWER (BLOOD FLOW TO THE BRAIN), DO SOME BREATH WORK AT THE BEACH OR AT A PARK, BAREFOOT. (GROUNDING), (IF YOU CANNOT LEAVE YOUR HOME) DO YOUR BREATH WORK ON YOUR BALCONY OR ON A MAT IN YOUR TV ROOM, BAREFOOT, JOURNAL ALL YOUR ANXIOUS THOUGHTS, GET THEM ON PAPER (IF THIS IS TOO TRIGGERING, SCRIBBLE RAPIDLY IN A JOURNAL FOR RELEASE), DO YOUR INNER-CHILD WORK.

ONCE COMPLETE, TURN ON THE COMEDY CHANNEL.

OFTEN ANXIETY IS JUST OUR BODIES ASKING FOR SOMETHING. THIS ROUTINE ALLOWS YOU TO TRIAL MULTIPLE SKILLS AND TOOLS. IT MAY JUST HELP YOUR ANXIETY GO FROM A TEN TO A SIX.

---

Affirmation: I choose to get up and help myself today.

SPRINKLE RESILIENCE ALL OVER THE PLACE LIKE FAIRY DUST BEFORE LIFE FORCES YOU TO.

---

HARD TIMES ARRIVE FOR US ALL. THIS IS NOT THE ISSUE. THE ISSUE IS BELIEVING YOU'RE INVINCIBLE TO LIFE'S CIRCUMSTANCES. THUS, YOU'RE COMPLETELY UNPREPARED WHEN A TORNADO HITS.

---

Affirmation: I choose to create a resilient mind through healthy habits.

REWIRING YOUR BRAIN AFTER TRAUMA IS A GIFT. YOU'VE JUST BEEN HANDED A PAINT BRUSH AND A BLANK CANVAS. YOU ARE FINALLY THE ARTIST OF YOUR OWN STORY.

---

GO ON, PAINT YOURSELF LIKE ALL OF YOUR ROLE MODELS ARE ONE. IT MAY BE A HUGE JOB, A LONG JOB OR YOUR NEW FULLTIME JOB. IT REQUIRES YEARS OF PATIENCE AND PRACTICE BUT IT IS ALSO THE JOB THAT WILL CHANGE EVERY SINGLE OUTCOME IN YOUR LIFE FOR THE BETTER. CHOOSE TO PAINT A BEAUTIFUL MIND.

---

Affirmation: I choose to illustrate a masterpiece through the art of rebirth.

THIS IS THE YEAR WE TAKE UP SPACE.

---

NO MORE APOLOGISING FOR BEING IN A ROOM WE DESERVE TO BE IN. NO MORE PEOPLE-PLEASING FOR THEIR COMFORT. THIS IS MY TURF. THIS IS MY TIME. THIS IS MY BIRTHRIGHT AND THIS MINDSET IS NON-NEGOTIABLE.

---

Affirmation: I choose to fill space.

## THE GRIEF OF OTHERS CAN EASILY BE A CONTAGION TO AN EMPATH.

---

PLEASE BE MINDFUL OF TAKING ON THE EMOTIONAL WEIGHT OF YOUR LOVED ONES. CARRYING THIS WILL NOT FIX THE SITUATION, NOR WILL IT HEAL THEM. IT WILL SIMPLY PAVE THE WAY FOR MORE SICK PEOPLE. THIS IS NOT SELFISH. IT IS SELFLESS. YOU'RE NO GOOD TO ANYONE IF YOU'RE UNSTABLE.

---

Affirmation: I choose to support loved ones and not let their grief become my own.

MY DEDICATION TO REALIGNMENT IS THE VERY THING THAT WILL ATTRACT EVERYTHING I DESIRE.

---

THERE IS NOTHING MORE ATTRACTIVE THAN SOMEONE RADIATING THEIR PEACE INTO THE UNIVERSE.

---

Affirmation: I choose to attract my desires by being all I desire.

# MAYBE YOU'RE NOT NEEDY, MAYBE YOU'VE JUST NEVER FELT SEEN.

---

FEELING SEEN GOES HAND-IN-HAND WITH HAVING THE COURAGE TO BE SEEN. LOVE YOURSELF AND YOU'LL BEGIN TO UNBURY THE COURAGE REQUIRED TO BARE YOURSELF. IT'S TIME YOU MAKE YOUR DEBUT ON THE STAGE OF VISIBILITY.

---

Affirmation: I choose to show myself.

THERE'S A WOUND. LOCATE IT. ISOLATE IT. LOOK AT IT. UNDERSTAND IT. NOURISH IT. LOVE IT. HEAL IT.

---

AND REPEAT.

---

Affirmation: I choose to take necessary steps toward my best self.

CHOOSE YOURSELF. IF THEY DENY YOUR SELF-EXPRESSION BY PLANTING SEEDS OF FEAR AROUND YOUR AUTHENTICITY, THEN THEY HAVE JUST BECOME YOUR BULLY.

---

DON'T LET THE BULLIES GET TO YOU.

---

Affirmation: I choose to be uncaged.

## THE WORLD NEVER CHANGED FROM LISTENING TO YOUR PARENTS.

---

IT IS YOUR JOB TO DISOBEY YOUR PARENTS. FALL, CRY, LEARN, GROW, EVOLVE, UNDERSTAND, PUSH BOUNDARIES AND FIGHT TO BE FULL OF YOUR TRUTH. THAT'S WHY YOU'RE HERE. YOU ARE NOT YOUR PARENTS AND THAT SHOULD NEVER BE YOUR GOAL. YOU ARE YOURS. YOU BELONG TO YOU.

---

Affirmation: I choose to disobey all rules placed upon me that do not feel genuine to myself.

OFTEN A WOUND IS JUST A HURDLE YOU CONTINUOUSLY TRIP OVER UNTIL YOU HAVE THE PATIENCE TO VIEW IT WITH A GENTLE GAZE AND THE YEARNING TO TRULY UNDERSTAND IT.

---

THE FIRST STEP IS BREATHING. THE SECOND STEP IS ASKING YOURSELF, "WHAT IS REALLY GOING ON HERE?" THERE IS ONLY ONE RULE – HONESTY AND COMPASSION ARE A MUST. DIG DEEP, DETECTIVE.

---

Affirmation: I choose intrigue over repeated behaviour.

SPOILER ALERT: YOUR OVERREACTION TO SOMETHING MINOR IS PAST PAIN RESURFACING.

---

TAKE THE TIME TO UNDERSTAND THE REAL WOUND BEING LAID AT YOUR FEET. IT IS UNHEALED, NEEDS YOUR ATTENTION AND IS OFTEN FROM CHILDHOOD.

---

Affirmation: I choose to therapise my large nervous system responses.

## HOW TO FIND LOVE

---

STEP 1: LOVE YOURSELF.
STEP 2: ATTRACT.
STEP 3: THERE SHOULD BE NO
STEP 3 IF YOU DID STEP 1 CORRECTLY.

---

Affirmation: I choose to attract great love.

DECLINING YOUR NEEDS GENERATES SELF-LOATHING, WHICH GENERATES VIOLENCE.

---

THE FIRST STEP TO WORLD PEACE IS NAMING AND CHASING WHAT YOU KNOW YOUR HEART YEARNS FOR.

---

Affirmation: I choose to chase what is rightfully mine.

MAYBE THEY'RE NOT
BAD, MAYBE THEY JUST
DID A BAD THING.

---

PEOPLE WITH MASS PAIN ARE
NOT WIRED TO MAKE THE RIGHT
CHOICES. THIS IS SCIENCE. CHOOSE
FORGIVENESS WHERE YOU CAN.
THE ALTERNATIVE IS NOT AS FREEING.

---

Affirmation: I choose to show compassion,
even when it seems impossible.

## YOU CAN FORGIVE ABUSIVE PARENTING STRATEGIES WHILE ALSO DEMANDING CHANGE AND RESPECT FOR NEW BOUNDARIES.

---

ALL PARENTS WILL MESS UP THEIR CHILDREN IN SOME WAY. IT IS INEVITABLE. THIS IS NOT AN ATTACK ON PARENTS. WE ARE ALL CHILDREN TO SOMEONE. MOST PARENTS DO THE BEST THEY CAN. A LOT TRY TO DO DIFFERENTLY FROM THEIR PARENTS. THERE IS, HOWEVER, SO MUCH YOU SUBCONSCIOUSLY PICK UP AND PASS DOWN TO YOUR CHILDREN. I THINK IT IS REALLY IMPORTANT TO UNDERSTAND WHAT WAS PASSED DOWN TO YOUR PARENTS AND TO SET CLEAR BOUNDARIES TO AVOID ANY FUTURE PAIN. PLEASE REMEMBER: IT NEVER HAD ANYTHING TO DO WITH THE CHILD'S WORTH OR IDENTITY. IT HAD EVERYTHING TO DO WITH THE PARENT'S FEAR OF OPENING THEIR EYES TO BOTH THEIR CHILD'S TRAUMA AND THEIR OWN.

---

Affirmation: I choose to forgive and make healthy change.

TODAY, I WILL VIEW THE WORLD THROUGH A LENS OF LOVE.

---

BECAUSE THERE ISN'T ENOUGH OF IT.

---

Affirmation: I choose to live simply and kindly.

PLEASE NEVER FORGET THAT YOU ALWAYS HAVE A CHOICE.

---

DIFFICULT TIMES REALLY REQUIRE YOU TO REMEMBER THIS, SO I'LL SAY IT AGAIN: YOU ALWAYS HAVE A CHOICE. CHOICE LIES IN YOUR REACTION, HOW PROACTIVE YOU ARE, WHERE YOU LAY YOUR FOCUS, YOUR HOPE, YOUR FAITH AND YOUR ABILITY TO SEE THE SILVER LINING.

---

Affirmation: I choose to be a soldier in the hardest of times.

NOTICE EVERY ONE OF YOUR THOUGHTS AND ACTIONS. GET RID OF THE ONES THAT BETRAY SELF-LOVE AND AMPLIFY THE ONES THAT IGNITE IT.

---

SELF-LOVE LOOKS SO SEXY ON YOU.

---

Affirmation: I choose high self-esteem.

THERE'S A FINE LINE BETWEEN 'I'M TRYING TO PROTECT YOU' AND 'I'M TRYING TO SUPPRESS YOU'.

---

KNOW THEIR INTENTION, THEN UNDERSTAND YOUR POWER AND CAPABILITY TO LET GO OF THEIR DESIRES FOR YOU. FOLLOW YOUR HEART'S NATURAL GRAVITATIONAL PULL. THE HEART IS INCAPABLE OF LYING.

---

Affirmation: I choose to politely decline the expectations of others regarding who I should be.

THE MIND CAN BE TAINTED
BY NEGATIVE EXPERIENCES
BUT THE HEART CANNOT.

---

WHEN YOUR MIND FEELS FOGGY
AND ALL CONSUMED, RELY ON YOUR
HEART TO BE FOREVER TRUTHFUL.

---

Affirmation: I choose to acknowledge
my heart's words when my mouth
is only capable of mumbling.

ARTISTRY LIVES IN THE CRACKS OF MY MIND. BROKENNESS IS A SPACE WHERE WE CAN ALLOW OURSELVES TO FEEL AND THRIVE IN CREATIVITY.

---

MAYBE IT'S TIME I WROTE A POEM, A MELODY, A VERSE OR A SONNET. WHATEVER IT MAY BE, IT WILL BE TRUTHFUL AND IT WILL BE MINE.

---

Affirmation: I choose expression in times of suffering.

MAYBE THE DEFEAT YOU'RE FEELING IS REALLY JUST A DEEPER SENSE OF PRESENCE.

---

A MENTAL HEALTH CRISIS WILL FORCE YOU TO GET IN TOUCH WITH YOUR EMOTIONS; POTENTIALLY FOR THE FIRST TIME. THIS IS INCREDIBLY OVERWHELMING. YOU ARE EAGERLY LEARNING TO DRIVE AUTOMATICALLY. BE GENTLE WITH YOURSELF.

---

Affirmation: I choose to be emotional and alive.

WHEN WE DIG DEEPER INTO NEW DEPTHS OF OUR DEPRESSION, WE FIND GOLD.

---

THIS WHIRLWIND OF THOUGHTS CAN BE EXHAUSTING TO SIT IN BUT WHEN YOU CORNER YOUR PAIN, IT HAS NO CHOICE BUT TO REDIRECT YOU TO YOUR LIFE'S PURPOSE. IT WILL ALL BECOME CLEAR.

---

Affirmation: I choose to keep digging until I find gold.

I WILL NOT TELL A STORY OF HOW I WAS ABUSED. IT IS NOT MY STORY TO TELL. IT IS THE ABUSER'S. MY STORY IS OF MY RESILIENCE, POWER AND UNDENIABLE ABILITY TO BOUNCE BACK IN SPITE OF.

---

I OWN THAT SHIT. THE REST IS YOURS TO SORT THROUGH.

---

Affirmation: I choose to write my own ending.

IF I SHARE SOMETHING WITH YOU IN CONFIDENCE, YOU HAVE NO RIGHT TO DISPOSE OF MY TEARS SIMPLY BECAUSE YOU CANNOT RELATE OR FEEL SILENCED.

---

THIS IS NOT ABOUT YOU. HAND OVER THE MIC. IT IS THEIR TURN.

---

Affirmation: I choose to stop and listen when someone shares their pain.

STOP GIVING OTHERS PERMISSION TO DRENCH YOU IN THEIR ARTICULATE POISON. WE ARE DONE DROWNING IN NEGATIVE WORDS.

---

MY FIRST PRIORITY IS NOT YOUR SATISFACTION, IT IS MY HEALING.

---

Affirmation: I choose to repudiate what feels harmful and unhelpful.

IF THEY HAVE NOT DEALT WITH THEIR OWN TRAUMA, THEY ARE CERTAINLY NOT QUALIFIED TO PATRONISINGLY THERAPISE YOU.

---

I HAVE NEWS FOR YOU; YOU NEED THERAPY. YES, YOU. YOU ARE HUMAN. YOU ARE NO DIFFERENT FROM OTHERS. YOU CANNOT WALK THROUGH THIS LIFE UNTOUCHED AND YOU DON'T DESERVE TO WALK THROUGH IT WHILE SUFFERING AND SUPPRESSING. IT IS UP TO YOU IF YOU CHOOSE TO HURT OR HELP OTHERS WITH YOUR PAIN. DOING NOTHING IS A CHOICE.

---

Affirmation: I choose to no longer soak up the words of unhealed people.

MAY I CHOOSE TO NOURISH MY CREATIVITY INSTEAD OF FALLING INTO CONFORMITY.

---

CONFORMING IS THE RESULT OF CONDITIONING. YOU ARE ALLOWED TO WANT SOMETHING DIFFERENT FOR YOURSELF. LISTEN CLOSELY TO YOUR MIND AND YOUR HEART'S WISHES.

---

Affirmation: I choose to break free.

## THINGS TO NORMALISE:

---

CHOOSING YOURSELF, LOVING YOUR FLAWS, RISKING IT ALL, SMILING THROUGH HARD TIMES, LOVING YOUR BODY, GETTING RID OF SEXUAL SHAME, PRIORITISING DOING NOTHING, JAZZ MUSIC IN THE MORNING, CARBS FOR DINNER.

WE ARE HUMAN, THEREFORE WE ARE IMPERFECT AND STILL MERIT INNER PEACE.

---

Affirmation: I choose to let go of anything that doesn't resemble love.

IT IS TIME TO TRULY LISTEN TO OUR INNER-CHILD'S VOICE INSTEAD OF HABITUALLY SILENCING IT.

---

IT MAY BE SOFT. IT MAY NOT ALWAYS BE WHAT WE WANT TO HEAR BUT IT IS ALWAYS TRUTHFUL AND WILL ALWAYS TELL YOU WHAT YOU NEED TO HEAR.

---

Affirmation: I choose not to cover my ears to my inner knowing.

## HAVE A CONVERSATION WITH A HOMELESS PERSON.

---

YOU MAY LEARN SO MUCH. YOU MAY MAKE THEIR DAY. YOU MAY ALSO STRESS A LITTLE LESS WHEN THEY WAKE YOU UP TO REALISE HOW BLESSED YOU ARE.

FRIENDLY REMINDER: YOU ARE NOT ABOVE THE HOMELESS. YOU WERE JUST LUCKIER THAN THEY WERE.

---

Affirmation: I choose to help those in need.

## INSTRUCTIONS ON HOW TO BE COOL:

---

DROP THE EGO, BUY YOUR MUMMA FLOWERS, LEARN FROM YOUR CHILDREN, ADMIT YOU DON'T HAVE THE ANSWERS, SPONSOR A CHILD, HAVE FRIENDS FROM ALL DIFFERENT ETHNICITIES, CHOOSE EQUALITY, DO SELF-CARE, BE HAPPILY SINGLE.

---

Affirmation: I choose radical coolness.

HOW LOUD DO I HAVE TO YELL, "I AM IN PAIN" FOR YOU TO FIND THE COURAGE TO LOVE ME IN THE WAY I NEED.

---

I AM STILL COMING TO TERMS WITH THE FACT THAT PEOPLE LOVE DIFFERENTLY AND THAT THEIR "I LOVE YOU SO MUCH, I COULDN'T BREATHE WITHOUT YOU," IS SOMETIMES DISGUISED AS WAFFLES IN BED.

---

Affirmation: I choose to unravel and accept the hidden 'I love you'.

I'M HEALING MYSELF,
FOR MYSELF AND FOR
THOSE I LOVE MOST.

---

I WILL LEAD BY EXAMPLE AND SHOW YOU WHAT SELF-LOVE LOOKS LIKE. YOU MAY NOT HAVE THE TOOLS TO SPEAK YOUR TRUTH JUST YET BUT I AM WILLING TO LEARN, MASTER AND TEACH. I AM DOING THIS FOR US.

---

Affirmation: I choose to fight for my friends and family lineage.

THE TRUTH IS THAT YOU CAN CHOOSE IF YOU WOULD RATHER SUPPRESS AND DWELL IN MEDIOCRITY FOR ETERNITY OR FIGHT TO KNOW YOURSELF.

---

KNOWING YOURSELF CAN BE SCARY. YOU PROBABLY WON'T LIKE ALL OF YOU. BUT HOW DO YOU EXPECT TO FALL IN LOVE WITH YOURSELF IF YOU DON'T LOOK AT YOUR OWN FLAWS THROUGH GENTLE EYES AND SEE THEM FOR WHAT THEY REALLY ARE – A HURTING CHILD STRUGGLING TO BELIEVE THEY ARE ENOUGH.

---

Affirmation: I choose to hold my inner child close to my heart and tell them all they long to hear.

AS LONG AS YOU'VE MADE THE DECISION TO STAY IN RECOVERY, A RELAPSE IS NOT AN ISSUE.

---

YOU ARE HUMAN. YOU ARE NOT A ROBOT. YOUR HEALING WILL NEVER BE LINEAR. DO NOT STOP UNTANGLING NOW. DO NOT WITHDRAW YOUR PROGRESS AND EVACUATE RIGHT BEFORE YOU REACH GOLD.

---

Affirmation: I choose to keep going.

IT IS BETTER TO FEEL EVERYTHING THAN TO HAVE NEVER FELT AT ALL.

---

I ADMIT, SOMETIMES I JUST WANT TO SIT BACK WITH A COFFEE AND NOT FEEL SO INTENSELY. BUT THAT IS EQUIVALENT TO LIVING A LIFE, DRINKING EVERYTHING AT HALF STRENGTH. IT IS NOT TRULY LIVING. NOW, I MAY FEEL MY GRIEF AT FULL STRENGTH BUT THE SWEETNESS OF MY JOY HAS THE ABILITY TO OVERPOWER ITS BITTERNESS.

---

Affirmation: I choose to spin the idea that my sensitivity is my greatest weapon.

I WILL LOVE MYSELF THE
SAME WAY A HEALED MOTHER
LOVES HER NEWBORN.

---

THIS IS AN EXAMPLE OF
UNCONDITIONAL, PURE LOVE.
THE KIND OF LOVE THAT CURES. I WILL
CHOOSE THIS EVERY DAY FOR MYSELF
BECAUSE I KNOW I AM DESERVING.

---

Affirmation: I choose to love
myself with no conditions.

I WILL GLADLY ABANDON YOUR DESIRES FOR ME BEFORE I ABANDON MYSELF AGAIN.

---

IF YOU PLACE AN EXPECTATION ON ME THAT CONTRASTS WITH MY IDENTITY, YOU HAVE MISUNDERSTOOD ME, MY CAPABILITIES, MY POWER AND MY INDESTRUCTIBLE SENSE OF SELF. YOU HAVE OUTSTAYED YOUR WELCOME. YOU ARE DEMOTED.

---

Affirmation: I choose to cast aside cruel expectations placed upon me.

I USED TO DESPISE SUFFERING. NOW, I SEE IT ARRIVES AT MY DOOR EACH TIME I HAVE ABANDONED MYSELF.

---

SUFFERING IS THE GREATEST GIFT ONE CAN RECEIVE. A BIT LIKE THIS BOOK, IT IS AN INVITATION TO RETURN. NEVER TRY TO SAVE SOMEONE FROM THEIR SUFFERING. LET THEM FEEL IT ALL. I GUARANTEE THE OUTCOME WILL BE TREMENDOUSLY REWARDING.

---

Affirmation: I choose to embrace suffering and discover what needs aid while in its depths.

YOU STOLE THE SPARK FROM MY EYES. YOU HURT THE SMALL CHILD WITHIN ME AND TOOK AWAY HIS INNOCENCE. YOU SWALLOWED MY SOUL. YOU TOOK WHAT YOU WANTED. YOU TOOK IT ALL.

---

I LOOK INTO THE SKY WITH A NARROW-EYED GAZE. I SEE GREY. YOU MADE IT ALL DULL AND QUIET.

BUT I STILL BELIEVE IN LOVE. I STILL BELIEVE THE NEXT ONE WILL BE BEAUTIFUL. SO, I PICK MYSELF BACK UP AND REMIND MYSELF THAT EVERY EXPERIENCE IS DIFFERENT.

---

Affirmation: I choose not to let past experiences dictate future outcomes.

YOU HAVE BEEN STRUGGLING WITH BELONGING YOUR ENTIRE LIFE. MAYBE YOU WERE NOT MEANT TO BELONG BUT, INSTEAD, INVITE.

---

YOU ARE DOING IT LIKE NO-ONE ELSE HAS. HAVE PRIDE. CREATE. INSPIRE. AND THEN WELCOME WITH OPEN ARMS.

---

Affirmation: I choose to let people belong with me.

SO MUCH CRYING BEHIND THESE FENDI GLASSES.

---

TAKE THEM OFF. FORGET THE IMAGE. THIS HIDING IS HURTING YOU TOO MUCH NOW.

---

Affirmation: I choose to drop all unhelpful facades.

SELF-LOVE SIMPLY MEANS RECOVERING ENOUGH TO RETURN TO YOUR WHOLE SELF.

---

IF YOU WANT TO TRULY LOVE YOURSELF, YOU NEED TO STOP LYING TO YOURSELF ABOUT WHAT NEEDS ACKNOWLEDGMENT INSIDE OF YOU. WE NEED TO RETRAIN OURSELVES TO CHECK IN AND START FEELING AGAIN. SEE WHAT CAUSES YOU PAIN AND RUSH TO ITS AID.

---

Affirmation: I choose to be honest with myself.

IF YOU LONG FOR FREEDOM FROM NUMBNESS AND ENTRAPMENT, YOU HAVE JUST ONE JOB – QUESTION YOUR CONDITIONING.

---

THIS CAN BE SCARY WORK. SCARY WORK WILL SET YOU FREE FROM A SYSTEM DEDICATED TO YOUR SUFFERING.

---

Affirmation: I choose to push through what is scary and foreign.

LIFE WILL ONLY PRESENT YOU WITH STRUGGLES AND HARDSHIPS IN AREAS IN WHICH YOU ARE NOT YET FREE.

---

HARDSHIP IS OPPORTUNITY. IT IS A GIFT. DO NOT REFUSE IT DUE TO ITS WEIGHT. EMBRACE, ACCEPT AND UNDERSTAND IT.

---

Affirmation: I choose to try something different in areas in which I am not yet free.

IT IS TIME WE BECOME BEST FRIENDS WITH OUR TRAUMA.

---

THE SOONER YOU START GETTING INQUISITIVE ABOUT THE PAIN INSIDE YOU, THE SOONER YOU WILL UNDERSTAND YOURSELF, HEAL YOURSELF AND STOP SUBCONSCIOUSLY PROJECTING THAT PAIN ONTO OTHERS. IT IS YOUR JOB, AS A HUMAN BEING, TO IDENTIFY WHEN YOUR TRAUMA IS LEADING THE CONVERSATION INSTEAD OF YOU.

---

Affirmation: I choose to love my trauma.

## IT'S CALLED LEMONADE, BABY.

---

I THANK YOU FOR THE ABUSE. YOU TOOK WHAT YOU WANTED BUT I TOOK WHAT YOU GAVE ME AND MADE IT THE ENERGETIC TO GET EVERYTHING I'VE EVER DESIRED.

---

Affirmation: I chose my outcome.

# ONE LAST NOTE

The biggest part of healing is peeling back the layers of hurt to discover which words are missing from your body and nervous system. These missing words are critical for us to make better and restore the damage life or current circumstances have permitted. This language must be said daily until you and your body believe it. I aspire for my words to resonate and treat my readers. I hope these words that healed me also heal you. We are all deserving of emotional stability. We all deserve to feel safe.

This book was my recovery. Recovery was with me every step of the way. He has been good to me. As I read over this book, I thought to rewrite a lot of it. I am still unsure if it will translate. I wrote so much while in the midst of excruciating mental pain; so far gone I am uncertain what I needed to say has even come out as English, let alone relatable or healing for others. I decided to leave it as it is. I will trust it will do what I aspire it to. I believe it is better this way – messy, unedited, rare, extreme, emotional, honest, large, confronting and maybe too much to hold at times. Because that is who we are when we are free. I am not small. I am not chill. I am alive. I am not relatable when I adapt, polish or over-polite myself for others. What I crave is real. What I need is to breathe freely.

What my entire being required was to intertwine my sensitivity with my need to help people.

I aspire for this book to inspire everyday people and to truly give even a glimmer of hope to those in the crux of a mental health crisis. You are the ones on the cusp of freedom. You need to hear you aren't alone on this journey. The ones who only see the option to check out – this messy book is truly yours. I love you. I know you. I feel you. I am always with you, showing you compassion, understanding the struggle and cheering you on every step of the way to your recovery.

You and I, we are special. We are the only ones who can save the world. We are so lost at times, yet so delicately daring. We are the ones who make great change. We can do the most difficult things. We are the most honest. We can't fall too far because, whether we like it or not, we have something too special inside us; something that decided this could never end badly. That decision was not up to you or me. You are my person and I am yours. We belong together. We are the ones capable of smiling the brightest. The world is so blessed to have us. I truly mean it when I say that it is an honour to have you here.

# SPECIAL THANKS

## To my friends:

Annalise Gasparre, Anne-Marie Cavaco, Chiara Patalano, Chloe Friedlander, Courtney Randell, Daniella Mirels, Emily Engeman, Georgia McCarthy, Isabella Forte, Katelin Koprivec, Kiarateuila Lattimore, Kimberley Anne Regent, Lauren Hollingworth, Maddy Varley, Sabrina Kirkham, Tom Lattimore.

Even if it was merely a kind word when I was down, I will not forget how you all showed up in your own way. It saved me. It meant everything to me in that moment. I will never stop having love for you. You are my people. You are my tribe. I am so happy we found each other.

## To my family:

Thank you for your patience. Thank you for your prayers. I love you more than anything.

## To my therapists and coaches:

You are good people. I respect you and your purpose so much. Thank you for being the logic that overpowered my instability.

## To my God:

Thank you for not answering my prayers for so long. I learned how to take matters into my own hands and be proactive in aligning every bit of me that was hurting. Courage now belongs to me. In all the pain, I discovered my need to dispose of any inauthenticity I was taught regarding faith. I finally know who *my* God is and I now know I can have it all.

## To my abuser:

You were so broken when I knew you. I am so sorry for what happened to you. Thank you for waking me up. I hope something wakes you up one day. Though that something will not be me, I am still praying for you.

## To my brave self:

You chose the ending to this chapter. You are my hero and my favourite person. It feels so good to love you again.

If you would like to order any of our Mental Health Packages or other products, such as our Inner Child Healing Cards and Daily Mental Health Checker Notepads, please visit www.abeautifulmindandco.com.au or visit our Instagram page, @abeautifulmindandco

I am also a trained performer and very passionate about the benefits music has on our mental and emotional health. I teach singing and acting. Whilst highlighting how trauma sits in the voice, I navigate my students toward unlocking their full resonance, which is often detained by their conditioning. If you would like to enquire about lessons, please visit: olivierssingingstudio.com.au or visit us on Instagram @oliviers_singing_studio.

Helping and coaching others is why I am here.

CPSIA information can be obtained
at www.ICGtesting.com
Printed in the USA
BVHW050044161222
654320BV00010B/791

9 780648 423096